D0169601

MITT ROMNEY

In His Own Words

EDITED BY

PHILLIP HINES

THRESHOLD EDITIONS

NEW YORK   LONDON   TORONTO   SYDNEY   NEW DELHI

Threshold Editions
A Division of Simon & Schuster, Inc.
1230 Avenue of the Americas
New York, NY 10020

First Threshold Editions trade paperback edition May 2012

THRESHOLD EDITIONS and colophon are registered trademarks
of Simon & Schuster, Inc.

For information about special discounts for bulk purchases,
please contact Simon & Schuster Special Sales at
1-866-506-1949 or business@simonandschuster.com.

The Simon & Schuster Speakers Bureau can bring authors to your live event.
For more information or to book an event, contact the Simon & Schuster Speakers
Bureau at 1-866-248-3049 or visit our website at www.simonspeakers.com.

Designed by Ruth Lee-Mui

Manufactured in the United States of America

1   3   5   7   9   10   8   6   4   2

Library of Congress Cataloging-in-Publication Data

Romney, Mitt.
Mitt Romney in his own words / [compiled and edited by] Phillip Hines.
p.   cm.
1. Romney, Mitt—Quotations.   2. Romney, Mitt—Political and social views.
3. Presidential candidates—United States—Quotations.
I. Hines, Phillip.   II. Title.
E901.1.R66A25   2012
974.4'044092—dc23   2012003844
ISBN 978-1-4516-8780-4
ISBN 978-1-4516-8781-1 (ebook)

To my loving parents,
Robert and Lucy

Acknowledgments

To Uncle George and Aunt Mary, without whom this book could not have happened. Thank you, George, for your help throughout this *entire* process.

To my superb agent, Scott Mendel, for taking me on, and for your great help.

To my editor, Karen Kosztolnyik, for your guidance and willingness to always help.

To my big brother, Jesse, for your expertise and help throughout this book, from the beginning to the end. Also, thank you for your significant help with the introduction.

To my little brother, Luke. You helped me out when I needed you most.

To my family and friends for your support along the way. Your encouragement is unquantifiable.

Contents

I'm not exactly sure how all this is going to work, but I think I'm going to get the nomination if we do our job right.

—Campaign event, Londonderry, New Hampshire,
December 27, 2011

Introduction

MITT ROMNEY:
THE INEVITABILITY OF ELECTABILITY

Because the Republican Party is intensely committed to defeating President Barack Obama in the 2012 presidential election, its primary focus is on finding and fielding a candidate who can beat him. Electability, rather than ideological purity, is the driving force behind Mitt Romney's consistent front-runner status in the GOP nominating contest.

Romney is the candidate best positioned to win the Republican nomination, and he comes across as the most serious challenger to President Obama in the general election.

Telegenic and articulate, Romney is both a successful businessman and a politician, with exceptional accomplishments in both careers. His pragmatic, moderate approach to both politics and policy brings with it a strong appeal to independent voters and disaffected Democrats, especially at a time when voters are deeply concerned about, and outright angry at, the persistently weak state of the economy.

In contrast to his many rivals for the GOP nomination, each one jockeying for position as the "anti-Romney" and pursuing the more conservative base, Romney has undeniable presidential presence: He is well versed in handling the media and is a formidable debater, having consistently held his own during the presidential debates.

However, he has also been one of the weakest front-runners for a party's nomination in recent political history, due in large part to Republican voters' preference for a more firebrand, philosophical conservative.

Romney has had to withstand surges by Michele Bachmann, Rick Perry, Herman Cain, Newt Gingrich, and Rick Santorum—each of them has arisen, one after the other, to assume temporary front-runner or co-front-runner status alongside Romney. Through it all, Romney has stuck to his presumptive-nominee approach—attack Obama while his opponents attack each other—and retained his perceived "inevitability of electability" aura.

ASSETS

Mitt Romney *looks* presidential. He is handsome, with a full head of dark, perfectly coiffed hair that's just ever so speckled with gray, despite his being sixty-five years old; he is tall, at six foot two. *People* magazine named Romney as one of its 50 Most Beautiful People in 2002. He bears a not-so-subtle resemblance to Ronald Reagan, the last great Republican president, a similarity that doubtless helps him with GOP voters.

Romney is intelligent, possessing an undergraduate degree in English from Brigham Young University and graduate degrees from both Harvard Law School and Harvard Business School.

Romney has had a very successful career in the private sector. In 1977, he began working for Bain & Company, a management consulting firm in Boston, Massachusetts. After having success at Bain & Company, he helped found the private equity investment firm Bain Capital, where he spent more than a decade in charge leading the firm in launching or rebuilding hundreds of companies, including Staples, Domino's Pizza, and the Sports Authority. In the early 1990's, Romney temporarily returned to Bain & Company when the company faced financial collapse. He successfully turned the company around, restoring profitability without cutting jobs.

Romney's business experience exemplifies his strongest

selling point: that he is uniquely qualified to help turn around America's economy and deal with out-of-control entitlement programs.

Further supporting the turnaround-artist case is Romney's success with the 2002 Salt Lake City Winter Olympics. In 1999, as the Games were about to collapse, running $379 million short of the projected revenues, Romney left Bain Capital again and took over as president and CEO of the Games. He helped the Games turn a profit of $100 million, as he directed a $1.32 billion budget, 700 employees, and 26,000 volunteers. Romney's role was so widely praised that he wrote a book about it, *Turnaround: Crisis, Leadership, and the Olympic Games.*

And there is Romney's record as governor of Massachusetts. As John Stimpson writes at FoxNews.com: "In 2002 [Romney] was elected governor of Massachusetts at a time when the state faced tremendous fiscal challenges. Despite taking office when there were just 23 Republicans in the 160 member House of Representatives and six Republicans in the 40 member Senate, he successfully restructured government programs, consolidated state services, reduced wasteful spending, and otherwise closed a $3 billion budget shortfall without raising taxes or borrowing from Wall Street."

As governor, Romney also enacted legislation that gained him substantial notoriety, for both good and ill: providing near-universal health care for Massachusetts citizens. While the state's mandate that everyone purchase health insurance is highly controversial and something that many GOP voters find reprehensible, RomneyCare has been successful, at least in terms of its ultimate goal. According to a November 2011 study by the The Blue Cross Blue Shield of Massachusetts Foundation, 98.1 percent of Massachusetts residents had health-care coverage, compared to the national average of 83.7 percent.

LIABILITIES

But Romney has liabilities, chief among them being that conservatives are skeptical about his fidelity to core conservative values. They see in Romney a Massachusetts moderate who will say whatever he thinks he has to in order to get elected, and he thus can come across more as a salesman for his candidacy than as a messenger of conservative orthodoxy.

At times, Romney's answers and statements regarding the exceptional nature of America and the superiority of the conservative philosophy can come across as bland and generic, chock full of as many right-wing buzzwords and catchphrases as he can muster. In other words, the fiery passion that is often tethered to a deep ideological vision, as is exhibited by Ron Paul, for example, has forever seemed missing in Romney. Hence his struggle to rouse exuberant support from conservative GOP voters.

One clear instance of this lack of clarity (as you'll see from the quotes in this book) is this: Last summer, Romney said he believes humans are contributing to global warming and that America should work to cut emissions, and then a few months later, he proclaimed that he doesn't know what is causing global warming and that spending lots of money to cut emissions is not wise.

Romney is also a Mormon, a minority faith viewed by many evangelical and fundamentalist Christians as a false religion; his Mormonism may also hurt him with liberal secularists, who abhor the traditional family values the faith exhorts and promotes.

Romney has reversed his position on abortion (though he likes to note that Ronald Reagan did as well), and as governor of Massachusetts, he instituted that controversial individual health insurance mandate program that his fellow GOP candidates are attacking as the basis for ObamaCare.

But, ultimately, even with those liabilities, Romney is still likely the best hope for the GOP to unseat President Obama.

MEET MITT ROMNEY

Mitt Romney in His Own Words is essential reading for voters who wish to better understand the candidate. This compilation of quotations sets forth Romney's actual views on every major issue, both personal and political, granting voters a true understanding of the candidate, without the distortion that often comes from the media and his opponents.

This book presents Romney's responses to criticisms he has received regarding his liabilities, as well as his actual views on specific policies. With more than 300 quotes from Romney on more than 150 topics taken from speeches, debates, interviews, his own writings, and other public utterances, it's a timely, handy book for voters who want to hear what Romney has to say and what he stands for.

Timeline

1947   Willard Mitt Romney is born in Detroit on March 12 to parents George and Lenore Romney. His first name comes from his father's best friend, J. Willard Marriott, the hotel magnate. His middle name is the nickname of Milton Romney, a quarterback for the National Football League's Chicago Bears from 1925 to 1929. Milton was a cousin of Mitt's father. George, born in Mexico, is a businessman who will later serve three terms as governor of Michigan.

1965   Starts dating fifteen-year-old Ann Davies after driving her home from a party; she is someone he has known since grade school.

1968   Almost dies in an auto accident while serving a two-and-a-half-year mission as a Mormon missionary in France.

1969   Marries Ann Davies. They will have five sons: Taggart (1970), Matthew (1971), Joshua (1975), Benjamin (1978), Craig (1981).

1971   Graduates from Brigham Young University with a bachelor of arts in English.

1975   Graduates from Harvard Law School and Harvard Business School.

1977   Begins working at Bain & Company, a management consulting firm in Boston.

1978   Named vice president of Bain & Company.

1984   Helps found venture capital firm Bain Capital.

1986   Becomes stake president for the Church of Jesus Christ of Latter-day Saints in the Boston region. He oversees several wards, or large congregations.

1991   Returns to Bain & Company as interim CEO and turns around the faltering company.

1992   Returns to Bain Capital.

1994   Steps down as stake president for the Church of Jesus Christ of Latter-day Saints in the Boston area.

1994   Unsuccessfully runs against Ted Kennedy for U.S. Senate in Massachusetts.

1996   Temporarily shuts down Bain Capital in search of a fellow executive's fourteen-year-old daughter, who had gone missing in New York City after attending a rave party. Romney leads a team of thirty people in conjunction with the police department, a detective, and his business partners. His efforts garner media attention. Romney's actions lead to the finding of the girl, in a basement in New Jersey, having overdosed on ecstasy and being just days from death.

1998   His wife, Ann, is diagnosed with multiple sclerosis.

1999   Leaves and retires from Bain Capital to become president and CEO of the financially troubled 2002 Winter Olympics Salt Lake Organizing Committee. Under his guidance, the Winter Olympics turns a profit of $100 million. Romney donates $1 million of his personal wealth and refuses to receive a salary unless the committee finishes in the black.

2002   Elected governor of Massachusetts with 50 percent of the vote.

2004   Publishes book *Turnaround: Crisis, Leadership, and the Olympic Games*.

2006   Signs historic Massachusetts health-care reform law.

2008   Unsuccessfully runs for president, coming in third overall to John McCain in the Republican primaries. McCain eventually loses in the general election to Barack Obama.

2010   Publishes book *No Apology: The Case for American Greatness*. It becomes a *New York Times* bestseller.

2011   Announces his candidacy for the 2012 presidential election. Despite being labeled a "moderate Republican" by many political and media pundits, he garners endorsements from respected Tea Party favorites, including Governor of New Jersey Chris Christie and Governor of South Carolina Nikki Haley.

1

DOMESTIC AND SOCIAL

I

DOMESTIC AND SOCIAL

ABORTION

I believe people will see that as governor, when I had to examine and grapple with this difficult issue, I came down on the side of life. I know in the four years I have served as governor I have learned and grown from the exposure to the thousands of good-hearted people who are working to change the culture in our country. I'm committed to promoting the culture of life. Like Ronald Reagan, and Henry Hyde, and others who became pro-life, I had this issue wrong in the past.

—*National Review Online*, December 14, 2006

Conservatives, of course, can make their own assessment. But the great thing is people don't have to look at what people say, they can look at what they do. When I was running for office 12 years ago, there were a number of things that I said and felt at that time that, with the benefit of experience, I have a different view today. One of those is abortion. As governor, I've had several pieces of legislation reach my desk that would have expanded abortion rights in Massachusetts. Each of those I vetoed. Every action I've taken as governor that relates to the sanctity of human life, I have stood on the side of life. So talk is cheap, but action is real. And people can now look at my record.

—*Human Events*, January 8, 2007

Abortion is taking human life. There's no question but that human life begins when all the DNA is there necessary for cells to divide and become a human being. Is it alive? Yes. Is it human? Yes. And, therefore, when we abort a fetus, we are taking a life at its infancy, at its very, very beginning roots, and a civilized society, I believe, respects the sanctity of human life.

—*This Week* with George Stephanopoulos,
ABC News, February 18, 2007

On being asked if women who have abortions and doctors who carry it out for them should go to jail: My view is that we should let each state have its own responsibility for guiding its laws relating to abortion. My preference would be to see the Supreme Court do something which is up to them, not up to me. Even if elected president, I don't guide this. The Supreme Court does. But I'd like to see the Supreme Court allow states to have greater leeway in defining their own laws.

—*This Week* with George Stephanopoulos,
ABC News, February 18, 2007

I was wrong. All right. I was effectively pro-choice when I ran for office. If people in this country are looking for someone who's never made a mistake on a policy issue and is not willing to admit they're ever wrong, why then they're going to have to find somebody else, because on abortion I was wrong. And I changed my mind as the governor. This didn't just happen the last couple of weeks or the last year. This happened when I was governor the first time a bill came to my desk that related to life. I could not sign a bill that would take away human life. I came down on the side of life every single instance as governor of Massachusetts. I was awarded by the Massachusetts Citizens for Life with their leadership award for my record. I'm proud to be pro-life, and I'm not going to be apologizing for people for becoming pro-life.

—GOP presidential debate, St. Petersburg, Florida,
November 28, 2007

I am pro-life and believe that abortion should be limited to only instances of rape, incest, or to save the life of the mother. I support the reversal of *Roe v. Wade*, because it is bad law and bad medicine. *Roe* was a misguided ruling that was a result of a small group of activist federal judges legislating from the bench.

—*National Review*, June 18, 2011

The law may call it a right, but no one ever called it a good. And in the quiet of conscience, people of both political parties know that more than a million abortions a year cannot be squared with the good heart of America.

—Values Voter Summit, Washington, D.C., October 8, 2011

As president, I'll end federal funding for abortion advocates like Planned Parenthood.

—Values Voter Summit, Washington, D.C., October 8, 2011

AIDS

As President, I will mobilize our civilian instruments of power to address HIV/AIDS, poverty and other challenges across Africa by empowering a single U.S. official with the responsibility and authority to lead all of America's civilian efforts in the region. I will fundamentally transform our international aid efforts so that more of our assistance goes to those suffering rather than bureaucracy. Today, only one-third of all foreign aid gets to the people it was intended to help. That must change.

—Press release, December 1, 2007

AMNESTY

I disagree fundamentally with the idea that the 12 million people who've come here illegally should all be allowed to remain in the United States permanently, potentially some of them applying for citizenship and becoming citizens, others just staying permanently. I think that is a form of amnesty and that is not appropriate.

—GOP presidential debate,
Manchester, New Hampshire, January 5, 2008

DEATH PENALTY

What we are doing is saying, for those people who oppose the death penalty—and there are a lot of them—some just oppose it on the basis they don't feel a government should ever take someone's life. But then there are others who say, look, I could support the death penalty, but I don't want to see innocent people being killed. And, in that case, we are saying, look, we are going to apply this law in very narrow circumstances, where there's torture involved or terrorism involved or mass murder. And we're going to have a standard of proof that's high enough that you don't have to worry about it being applied against the innocent. And so there has to be physical evidence, scientific evidence, and basically a jury saying, look, there is no doubt on this one. And take the Timothy McVeigh case or one that's local here [in Massachusetts], the Gary Sampson case, where multiple murders occur. In the case of Gary Sampson, there is a confession, where there is physical evidence. There's no question this person is guilty. And, in that kind of case, where there's been torture, mayhem, multiple murders, terrorism, these people ought to pay the ultimate price for their ultimate crime.

—*The Big Story* with John Gibson, Fox News Channel, May 2, 2005

EDUCATION

If we are going to compete in the global economy, we have to set our education goals higher. Gone are the days of a manufacturing-based economy when an eighth grade education was enough. The new millennium demands a higher educational standard for our children, and the speed with which we reach that standard will define the future of this country.

—Congressional testimony to the House Committee
on Education and the Workforce, May 17, 2005

We've found that most studies of successful schools—both district and charter schools—have five key criteria in common, and they're not going to surprise you. Good leaders, great teachers, data-driven decision-making, parent involvement, and high expectations for all students are at the top of every list.

—Congressional testimony to the House Committee
on Education and the Workforce, May 17, 2005

Teaching is less and less attractive to bright students fresh out of college—particularly in math and science—who are used to working in a team-oriented, performance-driven environment. Our schools today are set up in a manufacturing model, where teachers teach in isolation from their colleagues, aren't given the support or information they need to be successful, and have no opportunities for advancement or better pay unless they leave the classroom for administration. We've actually set up a system that discourages new teachers from coming in, and only provides incentives for the best teachers to leave the classroom. To attract and retain better teachers, we need to make teaching a profession again. We need to reward performance, and give teachers opportunities to take on new responsibilities without having to leave the classroom altogether.

—Congressional testimony to the House Committee
on Education and the Workforce, May 17, 2005

The 19th-century industrial labor-union model doesn't make sense for educating children. Teachers aren't manufacturing widgets. Better teachers should have better pay, advancement opportunities and mentoring responsibilities. Better pay should also accompany the most challenging assignments—needed specialties like math and science, advanced placement skills and extra effort.

—*Washington Times*, April 9, 2006

I proposed, at that time, for instance, that we eliminate the Department of Education. A lot of conservatives thought that was a great idea. I don't think that's a good idea anymore. I think we need the Department of Education. I think No Child Left Behind is performing a useful function in providing for testing. It has a lot of errors in it and I'd like to change it, but I like the fact that we're testing our kids.

—*This Week* with George Stephanopoulos,
ABC News, February 18, 2007

Our conservative agenda strengthens our family in part, by putting our schools on track to be the best in the world again. Because great schools start with great teachers, we'll insist on hiring teachers from the top third of college graduates and we'll give better teachers better pay. School accountability, school choice, cyber schools will be priorities and we'll put parents and teachers back in charge of education, not the fat-cat CEOs of the teachers' unions.

—Conservative Political Action Conference,
Washington, D.C., February 18, 2010

One, education has to be held at the local and state level, not at the federal level. We need to get the federal government out of education. And secondly, all the talk about we need smaller classroom size, look, that's promoted by the teachers' unions to hire more teachers. We looked at what drives good education in our state, what we found is the best thing for education is great teachers, hire the very best and brightest to be teachers, pay them properly, make sure that you have school choice, test your kids to see if they are meeting the standards that need to be met, and make sure that you put the parents in charge. And as president I will stand up to the national teachers' unions.

—GOP presidential debate,
Orlando, Florida, September 22, 2011

EMINENT DOMAIN

Well, I don't believe that land should be taken—the power of government to give to a private corporation. And so the right of eminent domain is a right which is used to foster a public purpose and public ownership for a road, highways, and so forth. And so my view is, if land is going to be taken for purposes of a private enterprise, that's the wrong way to go.

—GOP presidential debate,
Manchester, New Hampshire, June 13, 2011

EQUAL RIGHTS

Let me make it very clear: I am not a person who is anti-gay or anti–equal rights. I favor the treatment of all our citizens with respect and dignity. I do not favor creating a new legal special class for gay people. And I do not favor same-sex marriage, but as I've demonstrated through my own record, I have endeavored not to discriminate in hiring. . . . I believe that in America, we should not discriminate against people on the basis of our differences. But that doesn't mean that you create a law for every difference that exists between people. It opens the door to lawsuits.

—*National Journal*, February 10, 2007

FAMILY VALUES

When I was a little kid, there used to be the ditty that went around: first comes love, then comes marriage, then comes the baby in the baby carriage. Today that idea is foreign to some kids.

—*Charlie Rose*, PBS, June 5, 2006

Unfortunately, when it comes to marriage, our government's policies are often out of step with our values. If a couple have a baby, the government will actually give them more support—in the form of food stamps, welfare, or other benefits—than if they do not marry, than if they do. Our safety-net programs penalize the decision to marry, instead of rewarding it. That's just wrong. And that's why I'll eliminate these marriage penalties. And I will hold fathers financially responsible for their child, whether or not they married the mother.

—Values Voter Summit, Washington, D.C., October 8, 2011

GAMBLING

The last time the Legislature seriously considered an expansion of gaming in Massachusetts, we were facing a $3 billion budget deficit. Since then, we have closed the budget gap without raising taxes and without resorting to new forms of gaming. In fact, over the last two years, we have run surpluses in the hundreds of millions of dollars. I am not proposing, or even considering, an expansion of gaming. If someone were to bring forward a proposal, it is not something I would support given our economic circumstances and the social costs associated with gaming.

—*Boston Globe*, September 16, 2005

GUN RIGHTS

I'm not a big-game hunter. I've made it very clear. I've always been, if you will, a rodent and rabbit hunter. All right. Small varmints, if you will. And I began when I was, oh, fifteen or so and have hunted those kinds of varmints since then. More than two times. I also hunted quail in Georgia. So, I've . . . it's not really big-game hunting, if you will, it's not deer and large animals, but I've hunted a number of times, of various types of small rodents.

—Campaign event, Indianapolis, Indiana, April 5, 2007

But my position is we should check on the backgrounds of people who are trying to purchase guns. We also should keep weapons of unusual lethality from being on the street. And finally, we should go after people who use guns in the commission of crimes or illegally, but we should not interfere with the right of law-abiding citizens to own guns either for their own personal protection or hunting or any other lawful purpose.

—*Meet the Press*, NBC, December 16, 2007

I'm not going to describe all of my great exploits. But I went moose hunting actually—not moose hunting, I'm sorry, elk hunting with friends in Montana. I've been pheasant hunting. I'm not the great hunter that some on this stage, probably Rick Perry, my guess is you are a serious hunter. I'm not a serious hunter, but I must admit—I guess I enjoy the sport and when I get invited I'm delighted to be able to go hunting.

—GOP presidential debate,
Myrtle Beach, South Carolina, January 16, 2012

HOMELAND SECURITY

Well, of course we should be doing the same kind of intelligence work we have always done to protect ourselves from people who we think could be attacking us. And, in some cases, I'm sure the FBI infiltrates organizations they're concerned about. If they have probable cause, they're able to do wiretapping. And those are the tools that of course we use in protecting the homeland. What we need to do is more of that and have more resources devoted to the FBI in their effort to do intelligence work and counterintelligence work. We don't need different tools. We need to use the tools we have got under the Patriot Act and under our current laws to assure that we really are following groups that are preaching terror, that we really are following people who come here from terror-sponsored states, where that's appropriate, where we have concerns, that we have the resources necessary to prevent the bombs from going off, rather than just the resources to clean up afterwards.

—*The Big Story* with John Gibson,
Fox News Channel, September 15, 2005

IMMIGRATION

Let me make it real clear: I'm not anti-immigrant. I love immigrants. I love legal immigrants coming to our country. I'm happy to communicate to them. And I hope they vote for me.

—GOP presidential debate,
Manchester, New Hampshire, June 5, 2007

I was at the San Diego border and met with our Border Patrol agents. They told me that more than a half of those that try and come across those fences are able to do so. They said there's no way to stop them at the border, unless you close down the magnets. And the magnets are sanctuary cities and having employers sign people up that have come here illegally to do work here. You have to end sanctuary cities. You have to cut back on federal funding to cities that continue to call themselves sanctuary cities and welcome people in, as New York has done. And you have to say to employers that hire people illegally, "That's also going to be sanctioned." This is the way we're going to have to finally end it.

—GOP presidential debate,
Durham, New Hampshire, September 5, 2007

We're going to finally have a system that welcomes people here legally, and that says that those that have come here illegally are invited to get in line with everybody else. And the Constitution, as Senator [Fred] Thompson has indicated, indicates that those that are born here do become United States citizens by virtue of being born here. But if they're born here from parents who come across the border illegally and bring them here illegally, in my view, we should not adopt, then, these chain migration policies that say you've got a child here that's a U.S. citizen, and the whole family can come in. That, in my opinion, is a mistake. We are a nation of laws. And you're correctly going through each part of immigration policy here. But let's underscore this one more time: We are, in this audience, almost every person here, an individual who came to this country because it's a land of opportunity and liberty. We also, because we have laws, can have opportunity and liberty. We're going to enforce the laws. Welcoming people here—we're not going to cut off immigration; we're going to keep immigration alive and thriving. But we're going to end the practice of illegal immigration. It's not inhumane. It's humanitarian. It's compassionate. We're going to end illegal immigration to protect legal immigration.

—GOP presidential debate, Miami, Florida, December 9, 2007

Look, we are a nation of immigrants. We love legal immigration. But for legal immigration to work, we have to secure the border, and we also have to crack down on employers that hire people who are here illegally. I like legal immigration. I'd have the number of visas that we give to people here that come here legally, determined in part by the needs of our employment community. But we have to secure our border and crack down on those that bring folks here and hire here illegally.

—GOP presidential debate, Ames, Iowa, August 11, 2011

My friend Governor Perry said that if you don't agree with his position on giving that in-state tuition to illegals, that you don't have a heart. I think if you're opposed to illegal immigration, it doesn't mean that you don't have a heart. It means that you have a heart and a brain.

—Conservative Political Action Conference Florida,
Orlando, Florida, September 23, 2011

MARIJUANA

But having legalized marijuana is, in my view, an effort by a very committed few to try and get marijuana out in the public and ultimately legalize marijuana. It's the wrong way to go. We need less drugs in this society, not more drugs. And I would oppose the legalization of marijuana in the country.

  —Campaign event, Manchester, New Hampshire, October 4, 2007

MORMONISM

I just don't think Americans will do something the Constitution forbids. The Constitution says that there's no religious test shall ever be required for qualification to office in these United States. And I don't think my party or the American people would ever do that.

—*Charlie Rose*, PBS, June 5, 2006

There is part of the history of the church's past that I understand is troubling to people. Look, the polygamy, which was outlawed in our church in the 1800s, that's troubling to me. I have a great-great-grandfather. They were trying to build a generation out there in the desert. And so he took additional wives as he was told to do. And I must admit I can't imagine anything more awful than polygamy.

—*60 Minutes*, CBS, May 13, 2007

Commenting on Southern Baptist Theological Seminary president Al Mohler's concern that if he became the president, Mormonism would have "greater credibility" and hurt "evangelical missions": I hope everyone votes for the person they think can be the best leader for America. Each person is entitled to make his or her assessment. But I would note that my church is very demanding in terms of the requirements it places on people who join. It requires tithing 10 percent of gross income; abstinence from alcohol, tobacco, coffee, and tea; and [chastity] before and [fidelity] after marriage. I doubt very seriously anyone in the world is going to join my church simply because they see a leader who is a member of it. Even though I was governor of Massachusetts for four years, our chapel did not swell with supporters who wanted to join my church. Joining a faith is a far more serious matter than choosing something fashionable.

—*Christianity Today*, September 2007

Referring to people not voting for him because of his Mormon beliefs: I'm happy to have people ask questions. That doesn't bother me. And I think the reason that some 28, 29 percent are not comfortable voting for a Mormon is they think they're voting for Harry Reid. But that's not the case.

—*Face the Nation* with Bob Schieffer, CBS, October 21, 2007

The Bible is the word of God. I mean, I might interpret the word differently than you interpret the word, but I read the Bible and I believe the Bible is the word of God. I don't disagree with the Bible. I try to live by it.

—GOP presidential debate,
St. Petersburg, Florida, November 28, 2007

Almost fifty years ago another candidate from Massachusetts explained that he was an American running for president, not a Catholic running for president. Like him, I am an American running for president. I do not define my candidacy by my religion. A person should not be elected because of his faith nor should he be rejected because of his faith.

—"Faith in America" speech,
College Station, Texas, December 6, 2007

Let me assure you that no authorities of my church, or of any other church for that matter, will ever exert influence on presidential decisions. Their authority is theirs, within the province of church affairs, and it ends where the affairs of the nation begin.

—"Faith in America" speech,
College Station, Texas, December 6, 2007

There are some for whom these commitments are not enough. They would prefer it if I would simply distance myself from my religion, say that it is more a tradition than my personal conviction, or disavow one or another of its precepts. That I will not do. I believe in my Mormon faith and I endeavor to live by it. My faith is the faith of my fathers—I will be true to them and to my beliefs. Some believe that such a confession of my faith will sink my candidacy. If they are right, so be it. But I think they underestimate the American people. Americans do not respect believers of convenience.

—"Faith in America" speech,
College Station, Texas, December 6, 2007

There is one fundamental question about which I often am asked. What do I believe about Jesus Christ? I believe that Jesus Christ is the Son of God and the Savior of mankind. My church's beliefs about Christ may not all be the same as those of other faiths. Each religion has its own unique doctrines and history. These are not bases for criticism but rather a test of our tolerance. Religious tolerance would be a shallow principle indeed if it were reserved only for faiths with which we agree.

—"Faith in America" speech,
College Station, Texas, December 6, 2007

NATIONAL RIFLE
ASSOCIATION (NRA)

I support the work of the NRA. I'm a member of the NRA. But do we line up on every issue? No, we don't.

—*Meet the Press*, NBC, December 16, 2007

NEW MEDIA

The new media is a great force for the democratization of information. No longer can just a few newspapers or television stations control what information we have access to. The monopoly on news has been broken wide open. I trust the people and the power of ideas to triumph in the free and competitive information market that the new media provides.

—*National Review Online*, December 14, 2006

RELIGIOUS TOLERANCE

We ought to allow ceremonies, graduation ceremonies, and public events that we have the ability to recognize the Creator. I think it's appropriate for us to recognize the Creator in the public square. I think that having nativity scenes and menorahs in public places [during] the holidays is totally appropriate. I'm not looking for us to have prayer in the classroom every day or teachers leading in prayer. I don't think we should prohibit God from public places. I think "In God We Trust" belongs on our coin, and I think "under God" belongs in our pledge of allegiance.

—Campaign event, Carroll, Iowa, December 14, 2007

No, I think we recognize that the people of all faiths are welcome in this country. Our nation was founded on a principle of religious tolerance. That's in fact why some of the early patriots came to this country and we treat people with respect regardless of their religious persuasion.

—GOP presidential debate,
Manchester, New Hampshire, June 13, 2011

SAME-SEX MARRIAGE

Massachusetts should not become the Las Vegas of same-sex marriage. We do not intend to export our marriage confusion to the entire nation.

—*New York Times*, April 23, 2004

It's not right on paper, it's not right in fact. Every child has the right to have a mother and a father.

—Presidents' Day fund-raiser in
Spartanburg County, South Carolina, February 21, 2005

Like the vast majority of Americans, I've opposed same-sex marriage, but I've also opposed unjust discrimination against anyone, for racial or religious reasons, or for sexual preference. Americans are a tolerant, generous, and kind people. We all oppose bigotry and disparagement. But the debate over same-sex marriage is not a debate over tolerance. It is a debate about the purpose of the institution of marriage and it is a debate about activist judges who make up the law rather than interpret the law. I agree with 3,000 years of recorded history. I believe marriage is a sacred institution between a man and a woman and I have been rock solid in my support of traditional marriage. Marriage is first and foremost about nurturing and developing children. It's unfortunate that those who choose to defend the institution of marriage are often demonized.

—*National Review Online*, December 14, 2006

I believe that marriage is a status, not just an activity. As people move from state to state, that status would clearly carry with them. And, therefore, there needs to be a national standard. I believe that that standard ought to be the same as it's been from the beginning of recorded history, a relationship between a man and a woman.

—*U.S. News Digital Weekly*, June 12, 2009

SECULARISM

The attack on faith and religion is no less relentless. And tolerance for pornography, even celebration of it, and sexual promiscuity, combined with the twisted incentives of government welfare, have led to today's grim realities: 68 percent of African-American kids born out of wedlock, 45 percent of Hispanic kids, 25 percent of white kids. How much harder it is for these kids to succeed in school and in life. A nation built on the principles of the founding fathers cannot long stand when its children are raised without fathers in the home.

—Conservative Political Action Conference,
Washington, D.C., February 7, 2008

STEM CELL RESEARCH

Science must respect the sanctity of human life. The creation of life for destruction is simply wrong.

—Presidents' Day fund-raiser in
Spartanburg County, South Carolina, February 21, 2005

I believe that when a couple gets together and decides that they want to bring a child into the earth, and they go to a fertility clinic to do so, and if they're going . . . through that process [and have] a leftover embryo or two, that they should be able to decide whether to preserve that embryo for future use or to destroy it, to have it put up for adoption or potentially to be used for research and experimentation, hopefully leading to the cure of disease. And so for me, that's where the line is drawn. Those surplus embryos from fertility clinics can be used for research. But when we say we're moving into embryo farming, creating new life solely to experiment upon it and then destroy it, I believe we've gone across a very, very bright ethical line.

—*Fox News Sunday* with Chris Wallace,
Fox News Channel, May 22, 2005

The creation of new life specifically for the purpose of experimentation and destruction crosses a bright moral line. It is literally creating life to destroy it. And for me, whether that is done through embryo farming or done through cloning, both of them are wrong and are unacceptable.

—*Christianity Today*, September 2007

WELFARE

We know that the best welfare system isn't a handout but a hand up.

—Press release, July 8, 2005

2

ECONOMY

2

ECONOMY

BUDGET

Instead of thinking in the federal budget what we should cut, we should ask ourselves the opposite question: What should we keep? We should take all of what we're doing at the federal level and say, what are the things we're doing that we don't have to do? And those things we've got to stop doing, because we're borrowing $1.6 trillion more this year than we're taking in.

—GOP presidential debate,
Manchester, New Hampshire, June 13, 2011

I'm also going to immediately reduce the number of federal employees. That's something I can do directly. We'll dramatically cut back. And then something that needs legislative help, or approval, I am intent on linking the pay of government workers with the pay that exists in the private sector.

—Republican Jewish Coalition Presidential Candidates Forum,
Washington, D.C., December 7, 2011

BUSH TAX CUTS

The Bush tax cuts helped get our economy going again when we faced the last tough times. And that's why right now, as we face tough times, we need to have somebody who understands, if you will, has the private sector, has the business world, has the economy in their DNA. I do. I spent my life in the private sector. I know how jobs come and I know how they go, and I'll make sure that we create more good jobs for this nation. And one way to do that is by holding down taxes and making those tax cuts permanent.

—GOP presidential debate,
Boca Raton, Florida, January 24, 2008

BUSINESS

I specialize in turnarounds.

—*New York Times*, September 24, 2000

I'm proud of the fact that some of the companies we invested in created a lot of jobs. I had some failures, too. I know what it's like to have to make a tough decision. I've seen businesses go under. But I can tell you, I've been in the economy, I've been there in the real world, and we need a president who knows how the economy works, knows why jobs come and go, understands what the competition from China really means and how to stand up to it.

—GOP presidential debate,
Milford, New Hampshire, January 6, 2008

Now, I spent my life in the private sector, twenty-five years in business. I've traveled around the world in twenty different countries. I understand why jobs come and why they go. I'm not embarrassed to say that I was successful in that endeavor and I learned how to build businesses and create jobs.

—West Virginia Delegate Convention, February 5, 2008

The first rule in negotiation is if you're planning on giving up something that's important to you, make sure you get something that's more important to you from the other side. You don't give away your most valuable asset just because the other guy asked for it.

—*Human Events*, September 28, 2009

Having spent my career in the private sector, I know a thing or two about how jobs are created and how they are lost. The most important lesson I learned is that there are three rules of every successful turnaround: focus, focus, and focus.

—*Boston Herald*, March 8, 2011

I've not been in politics so long that I inhaled. I'm still a business guy.

—Republican Jewish Coalition, Las Vegas, Nevada, April 2, 2011

In response to a comment that his company bought ailing companies, improved them, and then sold "them at a net job loss to American workers": You know, that might be how some people would like to characterize what we did, but in fact, we started business at Bain Capital, and when we acquired businesses, in each case we tried to make them bigger, make them more successful and grow. The idea that somehow you can strip things down and it makes them more valuable is not a real effective investment strategy. We tried to make these businesses more successful. By the way, they didn't all work. But when it was all said and done, and we looked at the record we had during the years I was there, we added tens of thousands of jobs to the businesses we helped support. That experience, succeeding, failing, competing around the world, is what gives me the capacity to help get this economy going again.

—GOP presidential debate, Simi Valley, California, September 7, 2011

CARD CHECK

By tilting the playing field in favor of unions, card check not only robs workers of a secret ballot, it deprives management of the right to express its point of view. It will dramatically change the workplace as we know it, just as it's beginning to do for charter schools in Massachusetts. Small businesses will have to hire labor lawyers and follow burdensome new rules. If the parties can't agree on a contract, mandatory arbitration follows and employers that don't yield to union demands will have contracts foisted on them.

—*Washington Times*, March 25, 2009

CORPORATIONS

Corporations are people, my friend.

—Iowa State Fair, Des Moines, Iowa, August 11, 2011

Everything corporations earn ultimately goes to people. Where do you think it goes?

—Iowa State Fair, Des Moines, Iowa, August 11, 2011

EMERGING MARKETS

In the nineteenth century, the new frontier for us was the American West. In the twentieth century, it was Europe—selling products to Europe and North America. Now Asia has come out of poverty. A billion people who are steeped in poverty are coming out of poverty. They're consumers. We can sell products to them: medicines, technology, energy.

—GOP presidential debate,
Manchester, New Hampshire, June 5, 2007

ENTITLEMENT PROGRAMS

Right now federal spending is about 60 percent for entitlement—Social Security, Medicare, and Medicaid—and that's growing like crazy. It'll be 70 percent entitlements, plus interest, by the time of the next president's second term. And then the military is about 20 percent today. No one's talking about cutting the military. We ought to grow it. So people talk about the 20 percent and how we have to go after that 20 percent. There's not enough in the 20 percent to go after if we don't go after the entitlement problem. And you listen to all the folks running for president. No one wants to talk about it, but we have to talk about it. We have to put together a plan that says we're going to rein in the excessive growth in those areas, promising to meet the obligations we made to seniors. We're not going to change the deal on seniors but we're going to have to change the deal for twenty- and thirty- and forty-year-olds, or we're going to bankrupt our country.

—GOP presidential debate,
Simi Valley, California, January 30, 2008

FAIR TAX

There are a lot of features that are very attractive about a fair tax. Getting rid of the IRS is something we'd all love. But the truth is, we're going to have to pay taxes. We are the largest economy in the world. We've added, during the time Europe added 3 million jobs, we've added about 50 million jobs in this country. And so completely throwing out our tax system and coming up with an entirely new one is something we have to do very, very carefully.

—GOP presidential debate, Des Moines, Iowa, August 5, 2007

The idea of a national sales tax or a consumption tax has a lot to go for it. One, it would make us more competitive globally, as we send products around the world, because under the provisions of the World Trade Organization, you can reimburse that to an exporter. We can't reimburse our taxes right now. It also would level the playing field in the country, making sure everybody is paying some part of their fair share. But the way the fair tax has been structured, it has a real problem and that is it lowers the burden on the very highest-income folks and the very lowest and raises it on middle-income people. And the people who have been hurt most by the Obama economy are the middle class.

—GOP presidential debate, Tampa, Florida, September 12, 2011

FISCAL IRRESPONSIBILITY

You know for the last several years, we've been listening to liberals moan about $700 billion that have been spent over six years to win freedom in Iraq. They've now spent more than that in thirty days. We need to make it clear that with a government almost $12 trillion in debt, any unnecessary spending puts at risk the very creditworthiness of the United States. And if the world loses confidence in our currency, that could cause a run on the dollar, or hyperinflation that would wipe out savings and *devastate* the middle class. President Obama says he hopes to cut the deficit in half after four years. What does that mean? A deficit in 2012 of *$600 billion?* No president should accept such a staggering deficit, much less hold it up as a national goal. This is the time—as we're looking at these long-term budgets, this is the time where we're going to have to pare back government spending. It's not the time to fulfill every liberal dream and spend America into catastrophe.

—Conservative Political Action Conference,
Washington, D.C., February 27, 2009

America is not better off than it was $1.8 trillion ago.

—Conservative Political Action Conference,
Washington, D.C., February 18, 2010

This is a moral issue. To continuously spend and spend massively more than we're taking in is a real problem.

—*Your World with Neil Cavuto,*
Fox News Channel, March 3, 2010

FLAT TAX

Well, I'd love to see much flatter tax rates. I'd like to see us get rid of the special breaks. But one thing I can also say is I'm not looking for a way to take the top one percent of earners and have them pay a smaller share of the total burden. I want to make sure that the reduction is focused on the middle class. And I also want to make sure that every reduction we put in place creates the incentive for individuals to invest in the future, to build new jobs, to get good education, to go back to work.

—*The Kudlow Report*, CNBC, April 12, 2011

FREE MARKET

Criticizing President Obama's proposed stimulus bill, which eventually became the American Recovery and Reinvestment Act of 2009 and was signed into law by the president on February 17, 2009: In the final analysis, we know that only the private sector—entrepreneurs and businesses large and small—can create the millions of jobs our country needs. The invisible hand of the market always moves faster and better than the heavy hand of government.

—House Republican Conference Retreat, January 30, 2009

FREE TRADE

I'm not happy exporting jobs but we must move ahead in technology and patents. I don't like losing any jobs but we'll see new opportunities created selling products there. We'll have a net-net increase in economic activity, just as we did with free trade. It's tempting to want to protect our markets and stay closed. But at some point it all comes crashing down and you're hopelessly left behind. Then you are Russia.

—Forrester Research executive strategy summit,
Boston, Massachusetts, November 16, 2005

Well, I believe in trade, but I believe in opening up markets to American goods and services. And it's been calculated that the average family in America is $9,000 a year richer because we have the ability to sell products around the world. And a lot of people in this country make their living making products that go around the world.

—GOP presidential debate,
Dearborn, Michigan, October 9, 2007

GREAT RECESSION

There's so much blame that could be assessed that you'd say, look, Wall Street made mistakes. The S&P, the people that oversee the ratings agencies made mistakes, Congress made mistakes. They have oversight committees to look at these various areas. Also, in the administration there is something called the OFEHO, the Office of Federal Enterprise Housing Oversight. They weren't doing their job. A lot of people made mistakes. [Editor's note: The actual name is OFHEO, Office of Federal Housing Enterprise Oversight.]

—*The Situation Room with Wolf Blitzer,*
CNN, September 16, 2008

INVESTMENT

When I was at Bain Capital, we invested in about one hundred different companies. Not all of them worked. I know there are some people in Washington that doesn't understand how the free economy works. They think if you invest in a business, it's always going to go well. And they don't always go well.

—GOP presidential debate, Ames, Iowa, August 11, 2011

JOBS

Job and income growth can only come from a growing, successful private sector. Of course, government can create innumerable public sector jobs, but in doing so, it supplants the private sector and ultimately depresses the prosperity of its citizens. A pro-job, pro-prosperity government works to create the conditions that enable businesses of all sizes to grow and thrive. These should include aligning corporate taxes with those of other developed economies, eliminating special corporate tax breaks that lobbyists have inserted over the years, and preserving the Bush tax cuts—especially for small business.

—*USA Today*, August 18, 2010

NATIONAL
CATASTROPHIC FUND

The answer is yes, I do support some kind of national cata-strophic effort to make sure that people can get homeowner's insurance that protects them against flood or hurricane or tor-nado or whatever natural disaster might occur, or man-made disaster in some cases. We had the problem not just in Florida, but we also had the problem in Massachusetts. Those poor folks that are snowbirds that go from Massachusetts to Florida see it in both states, because people who live along the coast-line across the Atlantic have the same problem. Getting home-owner's insurance is oftentimes almost impossible. And so what we're going to have to do, as you just indicated, we're going to have to work together to create a program that gets people in high-risk areas insured. Now, I'm not in favor of saying that the people in Iowa should have to subsidize the people in Massa-chusetts or the people in Florida—that doesn't make a lot of sense—but to have those states that are in high-risk areas come together and say, "How do we organize an effort on a national basis that actuarially deals with the differences between differ-ent states and the different risks they face and make sure that we have a backstop behind the private insurance industry?"

—GOP presidential debate,
Boca Raton, Florida, January 24, 2008

NATIONAL DEBT

Our big government debt problem is not a Democrat problem—it is a Democrat and Republican problem. When President Bush and Republicans were in charge, they grew government, grew spending, and grew debt just like the Democrats. Neither party has been willing to say no to the people who want more and more from government. Saying yes wins votes. Saying no means concession speeches.

—*No Apology*, by Mitt Romney, 2010

PORK-BARREL SPENDING

Every bill that comes forward that's got pork in it and earmarks that are unnecessary, we've got to veto them and send them back. And that's a lesson that's going to have to be done. But it's got to be broader than that. We're going to have to see fundamental change in the way Washington works. We're just not going to get out-of-the-box thinking with inside-the-Beltway politics.

—GOP presidential debate,
St. Petersburg, Florida, November 28, 2007

PROFITS

Profits do not go into the pockets of executives. By and large they are reinvested in new technology and new ideas and growth. What you want to see is profits in corporations where those corporations invest in new technologies and new ideas. And that is our future.

—*The Kudlow Report*, CNBC, February 7, 2007

PROTECTIONISM

Protectionism sounds wonderful, which is the idea that we're going to protect our companies, our industry from foreign competition. But the other side of protectionism is that the people we trade with are not entirely stupid. If we say we're not going to let their goods and services in, they won't let our goods and services in. It works both ways. And one out of six jobs in this country is associated with sending goods and services to other countries. Export, in other words. And so you start talking protectionism, we're going to have an enormous job loss on the part of entrepreneurial businesses. Now, yeah, maybe some of the steel companies and auto companies would feel better for a while but not for very long because you put protectionist barriers up, it's going to hurt us and it's going to hurt everybody else.
— *The Glenn Beck Program*, November 3, 2008

THE RICH

I don't stay awake at night worrying about the taxes that rich people are paying, to tell you the truth. I'm concerned about the taxes that middle-class families are paying. They're under a lot of pressure. Gasoline's expensive. Home heating oil, particularly in the Northeast, is very difficult for folks. Health-care costs are going through the roof. Education costs and higher education are overwhelming. And as a result, we need to reduce the burden on middle-income families in this country.

—GOP presidential debate,
Johnston, Iowa, December 12, 2007

I'm not worried about rich people. They are doing just fine. The very poor have a safety net, they're taken care of. But the people in the middle, the hardworking Americans, are the people who need a break, and that is why I focused my tax cut right there.

—GOP presidential debate,
Hanover, New Hampshire, October 11, 2011

SMALL BUSINESS

Small companies in this country create the vast majority of jobs in America. I began a very small business that's grown. My business has not laid people off. It's grown and grown and grown.
—*Late Edition with Wolf Blitzer*, CNN, January 13, 2008

SOCIAL SECURITY

No, I don't want to raise taxes. I've pointed out that—that of the four ways to solve the shortfall in Social Security, the worst idea is to raise taxes on the American people, because it has a double—double whammy. Not only are you taking money away from their pocketbooks, you're also slowing down the economy. You slow down the economy, more people lose work. More people lose work, of course, you're having a lot of folks that really have their lives turned upside down. So, raising taxes is just something you don't want to do. There are three other ways that you can solve the problem of Social Security, and they're ways that have been brought forward by a number of Republicans over the years. We're going to have to sit down with the Democrats and say, let's have a compromise on these three elements that could get us to bring Social Security into economic balance. What are they? Well, number one, you can have personal accounts where people can invest in something that does better than government bonds—with some portion of their Social Security. Number two, you can say we're going to have the initial benefit calculations for wealthier Americans calculated based on the Consumer Price Index rather than the wage index. That saves almost two-thirds of the shortfall. And then number three, you can change the retirement age. You can push it out a little bit. And so those are the three arithmetic things you can do.

—GOP presidential debate,
Boca Raton, Florida, January 24, 2008

We have always had, at the heart of our party, a recognition that we want to care for those in need, and our seniors have the need of Social Security. I will make sure that we keep the program and we make it financially secure, we save Social Security, and under no circumstances would I ever say by any measure it's a failure. It is working for millions of Americans, and I'll keep it working for millions of Americans. And we've got to do that as a party.

—GOP presidential debate,
Simi Valley, California, September 7, 2011

Now, my own view is that we have to make it very, very clear that Social Security is a responsibility of the federal government, not the state governments, that we're going to have one plan, and we're going to make sure that it's fiscally sound and stable. And I'm absolutely committed to keeping Social Security working.

—GOP presidential debate,
Orlando, Florida, September 22, 2011

It would be a moral wrong to renege on the "iron-clad commitment" we have made as a society to our nation's elderly and vulnerable. The American people are looking to keep Social Security alive and well, and I believe the Republican Party should be committed to doing just that. If I am fortunate enough to be my party's nominee, I will advocate for solutions that keep Social Security strong for seniors now and in the future.

—*Foxnews.com*, September 22, 2011

STIMULUS BILL

This is a time to be very serious about helping build our economy. And spending hundreds of millions of dollars on contraceptives or hundreds of millions of dollars even on nice things like helping teenagers understand the risks of sexually transmitted diseases, this has nothing to do with economic stimulus.

—*Your World with Neil Cavuto*,
Fox News Channel, January 28, 2009

I think the Republican stimulus bill was better than the president's. His has a lot of waste in it. He seems to be unwilling to rein in excessive spending. His budget is a nightmare, and, as Senator Judd Gregg indicated, could bankrupt America. It's a huge mistake, in my view. But, the economy, that's going to turn around, always has, always will. The question is, will Barack Obama's plan have helped it or have hurt it?

—*The Situation Room with Wolf Blitzer*, CNN, April 21, 2009

He said, look, his stimulus plan would hold unemployment down to 8 percent and if we didn't pass his almost three-quarters-of-a-trillion stimulus we get a 10 percent unemployment. We got the 10 percent. Which pretty much shows the stimulus plan didn't do what it was designed to do.

—*Larry King Live*, CNN, December 3, 2009

SUBSIDIES

I believe in domestic supports for our agriculture industry. I don't want to see our food supply being the same kind of jeopardy situation that our energy supply is in. And clearly, there's a responsibility of government to make sure that our farmers are treated on the same basis as farmers in Europe and other markets that we compete with when [in] the middle of the Doha round at the WTO talks. And if we find a way to bring down subsidies around the world, that will be good news.

—GOP presidential debate, Dearborn, Michigan, October 9, 2007

TAXES

I believe it's critical for our economy going forward that we lower taxes again and we do so for the middle class. And so I've proposed a special savings plan for people in middle incomes. And that savings plan is this: Any interest income, or dividend income, or capital gains earned by people earning less than $200,000 a year should be taxed at the new rate of zero. Let people save their money for whatever purpose they'd like to save. I believe that will help stimulate our economy, create the economic base for growth of our new jobs, and make it easier for middle-income folks to make ends meet.

—GOP presidential debate,
Milford, New Hampshire, January 6, 2008

Is there anybody out there that thinks raising taxes would help the economy right now? I don't think so. I think everybody recognizes—even Barack Obama has said—he can't put in place tax increases until the economy gets stronger. That's a pretty clear indication even he recognizes that raising taxes right now would not help the economy. It would hurt it.

—*The Situation Room with Wolf Blitzer*, CNN, September 16, 2008

A smart tax system would reward investment, savings and entrepreneurship, while providing job-creators with the predictability and stability they need to grow our economy. But our tax system is not smart; it's quite the opposite.

—*Orlando Sentinel*, April 14, 2011

TAX LOOPHOLES

In my opinion, a loophole is when someone takes advantage of a tax law in a way that wasn't intended by the legislation. And we had in my state, for instance, we had a special provision for real estate enterprises that owned a lot of real estate. And it provided lower tax rates in certain circumstances and some banks had figured out that by calling themselves real estate companies, they could get a special tax break. And we said, "No more of that, you're not going to game with the system." And so if there are taxpayers who find ways to distort the tax law and take advantage of what I'll call loopholes in a way that are not intended by Congress or intended by the people, absolutely I'd close those loopholes. But, there are a lot of people who use the word loophole to say, "Let's just raise taxes on people." And that I will not do. I will not raise taxes.

—Iowa State Fair, Des Moines, Iowa, August 11, 2011

TROUBLED ASSETS RELIEF PROGRAM (TARP)

I know that we didn't all agree on TARP. I happen to believe it was necessary to prevent a cascade of bank collapses. For free markets to work, there has to be a currency and a functioning financial system. But we can agree on this: TARP should not have been used to bail out GM, Chrysler, and the UAW.

—Conservative Political Action Conference,
Washington, D.C., February 27, 2009

We have the TARP program, which has served its usefulness. The money that's left should be turned back either to reduce the deficit, or to pay for something of this nature.

—*Your World with Neil Cavuto*,
Fox News Channel, March 3, 2010

UNEMPLOYMENT
INSURANCE

A decent and humane society must have a strong safety net for the unemployed. I served for 15 years as a lay pastor in my church and saw the heartbreak of joblessness up close; a shattering loss of faith in oneself is but only one of many forms the suffering can take. Nonetheless, the vital necessity of providing for those without work should not be used as an excuse to ignore the very real problems of our unemployment system. In this, as in so many other arenas of government policy, unemployment insurance has many unintended effects. The indisputable fact is that unemployment benefits, despite a web of regulations, actually serve to discourage some individuals from taking jobs, especially when the benefits extend across years.

—*USA Today*, December 14, 2010

Unemployment benefits, I think they've gone on a long, long, long time. We have to find ways to reduce our spending on a lot of the antipoverty programs and unemployment programs. But I would far rather see a reform of our unemployment system, to allow people to have a personal account which they're able to draw from as opposed to having endless unemployment benefits. So, again, let's reform the system, make the system work better by giving people responsibility for their own employment opportunities and having that account, rather than doling out year after year more money from an unemployment system.

—GOP presidential debate, Ames, Iowa, August 11, 2011

UNEMPLOYMENT RATE

I'm afraid some people are becoming conditioned to unemployment rates above 8 percent. The idea that we celebrate 8.8 percent—I mean, my gosh!

—Event in North Las Vegas, Nevada, April 1, 2011

Unemployment is not a statistic. Unemployment is real pain and sorrow in the lives of a lot of people.

—Republican Jewish Coalition,
Las Vegas, Nevada, April 2, 2011

UNIONS

With regards to unions overall, there are some good ones and some not so good. The good ones are those that say how can we do a better and better job helping our members have better and better skills and making sure that the enterprises they work in are more and more productive?

—GOP presidential debate,
Dearborn, Michigan, October 9, 2007

Conservatives like me are opposed to card check, but not to unions. At their best, labor unions have always fought for the rights of workers, and generations of Americans have been better off for it.

—*Washington Times*, March 25, 2009

Referring to the Employee Free Choice Act, and how he believes it to be unnecessary: Labor unions play an important role in the American economy, and historically they have improved the lives of millions of workers. Today's labor laws already protect the rights of employees seeking union representation and bargaining collectively for contracts.

—*Denverpost.com*, August 7, 2009

U.S. AUTO INDUSTRY

But let me make a couple of points in this regard. One is we want the U.S. auto industry to survive, to grow, to thrive. Two is that if we just send money to Detroit and say, "Keep playing the game the way you have," that's not going to happen. What'll happen is the industry will decline and decline over the years until it doesn't exist anymore. So what is needed is the opportunity to dramatically restructure the costs of making cars by Ford, Chrysler, and General Motors. And for that to happen, you're going to have to have either a very powerful czar of some kind who can step in and open up contracts and change the basic structure of the industry, or go through a prepackaged, managed bankruptcy. The government is going to be part of this process either through the courts or through a super-powerful car czar, if you will. But business as usual is not the way to preserve these jobs and to build a brighter future for the many people who work in the auto industry. And by the way, as a son of Detroit—my dad was a CEO of a car company—I care very deeply about seeing this industry get restructured so that they can become resurgent and be a major employer for many, many years to come. There's no reason why Detroit can't play and win in the world market.

—*On the Record w/Greta Van Susteren*,
Fox News Channel, December 10, 2008

3

ENERGY AND ENVIRONMENT

ALASKA NATIONAL WILDLIFE REFUGE (ANWR)— DRILLING FOR OIL

Alaska is the easiest; the people of the state want us to drill there and the nation wants to drill there. Let's do it. But in this case the Democrats are listening to extreme environmentalists that say no.

—Campaign event, Muscatine, Iowa, December 13, 2007

ALTERNATIVE ENERGY

I love solar and wind [power] but they don't drive cars. And we're not all going to drive Chevy Volts.

—Campaign event, Manchester, New Hampshire, June 3, 2011

To begin with, wind and solar power, two of the most ballyhooed forms of alternative fuel, remain sharply uncompetitive on their own with conventional resources such as oil and natural gas in most applications. Indeed, at current prices, these technologies make little sense for the consuming public but great sense only for the companies reaping profits from taxpayer subsidies.

—Believe in America: Mitt Romney's Plan for
Jobs and Economic Growth, 2011

CAP AND TRADE

I do not believe in a cap-and-trade program. By the way, they don't call it "America warming," they call it "global warming." So the idea of America spending massive amounts, trillions of dollars to somehow stop global warming is not a great idea. It loses jobs for Americans and ultimately it won't be successful, because industries that are energy intensive will just get up and go somewhere else. So it doesn't make any sense at all.

—Campaign event,
Pittsburgh, Pennsylvania, December 27, 2007

I support it on a global basis as one of the possible solutions. I do not support it for the USA alone. I want to do it with other nations involved as a global solution.

—Campaign event,
Manchester, New Hampshire, October 27, 2011

CARBON

Unfortunately—or fortunately, as the case may be—carbon is the source of energy that drives our automobiles and a lot of our energy needs.

—*The Kudlow Report*, CNBC, April 12, 2011

I think we may have made a mistake—we have made a mistake is what I believe—in saying that the EPA should regulate carbon emissions. I don't think that was the intent of the original legislation, and I don't think carbon is a pollutant in the sense of harming our bodies.

—Campaign event, Derry, New Hampshire, July 14, 2011

I'm all in favor of eliminating pollution. Now, I know there is also a movement to say that carbon dioxide should be guided or should be managed by the Environmental Protection Agency. I disagree with that. I exhale carbon dioxide. I don't want those guys following me around with a meter to see if I'm breathing too hard.

—Campaign event,
Manchester, New Hampshire, November 18, 2011

COAL

Neither can we ignore coal as a substitute for foreign oil. Coal currently provides 48 percent of our electricity and 23 percent of our total energy. The United States has the largest coal reserves in the world, reserves that we can count on for the next 200 to 300 years. In addition to being used to generate electricity, coal can be liquefied and used as a transportation fuel. For those who see energy security as the primary goal of our energy policy, coal is an obvious answer. For those who are also concerned about warming, the challenge is that coal is one of the largest emitters of greenhouse gases of all energy sources.

We could overcome the challenge if we were able to capture the carbon dioxide from coal and store it away. Technology already exists—the coal capture and storage process is currently being employed in a small coal gasification plant in Beulah, North Dakota, which sends the carbon dioxide it emits not into the air but into a pipeline that travels north to Canada, where some of it is used for enhanced oil recovery and the rest is stored underground. Whether carbon dioxide from coal can be captured and stored by larger commercial facilities remains to be seen, but surely research and development of this technology should become a high priority for us and for other nations with large coal reserves like China, Russia, and the United Kingdom.

—*No Apology*, by Mitt Romney, 2010

CONSEQUENCES OF NOT DEVELOPING ENERGY RESOURCES

I think the president has to be, not just the commander in chief, but the communicator in chief and to talk to the American people about the consequences of not developing our resources. There are a lot of people that say we don't want nuclear power; okay. There are others that say we don't want to drill for oil; okay. If you don't want nuclear power, and you don't want to drill for oil, and you don't want clean-burning coal, then what that means is, hundred-dollar oil, then it's going to be, well, let's put it in gasoline terms: $3 a gallon, then to $5 a gallon, then to $8 a gallon, then $10 a gallon. And by the way, that means it's going to be some pretty tough living around here. And heating your homes, instead of costing, you know, $1,500 for a winter, it's going to be $3,000, and then $6,000. Those are the consequences, and [the president has to] show people this is what it means, but we have to make those decisions *today*.

—Campaign event, Muscatine, Iowa, December 13, 2007

ENERGY EFFICIENCY

I also want to see us become more energy efficient. I'm told that we use almost twice as much energy per person as does a European, and more like three times as much energy as does a Japanese citizen. We could do a lot better. I'd like to see us get our vehicles, and our homes, and our systems of insulation and so forth become far more efficient. I think that's happening and believe that we have a role in trying to encourage that to happen.

—Campaign event, Manchester, New Hampshire, June 3, 2011

ENERGY INDEPENDENCE

We use about 25 percent of the world's oil supply to power our economy, but according to the Department of Energy, we possess only 1.7 percent of the world's crude oil reserves. Our military and economic strength depend on our becoming energy independent—moving past symbolic measures to actually produce as much energy as we use. This could take 20 years or more; and, of course, we would continue to purchase fuel after that time. Yet we would end our strategic vulnerability to oil shutoffs by nations such as Iran, Russia, and Venezuela and stop sending almost $1 billion a day to other oil-producing nations, some of which use the money against us. (At the same time, we may well be able to rein in our greenhouse gas emissions.) Energy independence will require technology that allows us to use energy more efficiently in our cars, homes, and businesses. It will also mean increasing our domestic energy production with more drilling offshore and in the Arctic National Wildlife Refuge, more nuclear power, more renewable energy sources, more ethanol, more biodiesel, more solar and wind power, and a fuller exploitation of coal. Shared investments or incentives may be required to develop additional and alternative sources of energy.

—*Foreign Affairs*, July/August 2007

And we simply—even though I love solar and love wind, like most people do, I like the renewable sources—they alone are not going to get America energy independent. We spend almost a half a trillion dollars a year buying energy from other people. That's money that should be invested in our own economy. So yeah, should we drill? Sure. Should we also be using our natural gas resources? We just had this extraordinary gift given to us by finding technology that frees up about one hundred years of natural gas. Let's use the resources we have and use those resources at a time when we're developing some sustainable sources of energy that can help us further down the road.

—*The Kudlow Report*, CNBC, April 12, 2011

ENERGY POLICY

My view with regards to energy policy is pretty straightforward: I want us to become energy secure and independent of the oil cartels.

—Campaign event, Pittsburgh, Pennsylvania, October 27, 2011

ENERGY RESEARCH AND DEVELOPMENT

We spend about $4 billion a year right now on energy research to try and help us become more energy, or less energy dependent on foreign sources. Some of that is on developing new sources of energy; some is on developing efficiencies in automobiles, in homes, appliances, and so forth. And I think over the coming years we need to increase our investment to become energy independent from about $4 billion a year to about $20 billion a year. And that, obviously, has got to grow gradually because there are not a lot of places now that do the kind of research we need to do to get ourselves energy independent.

—*Fox News Sunday* with Chris Wallace,
Fox News Channel, January 20, 2008

ENVIRONMENTAL
PROTECTION AGENCY (EPA)

I believe we should keep our air and our water clean. And that we don't want to have pollutants that are interfering with our health and damaging the ability of our children to enjoy good health. So no question we have to have standards that improve the quality of our air. And I support reasonable standards. . . . Do I support the EPA? In much of its mission, yes, but in some of its mission, no.

—Campaign event, Derry, New Hampshire, July 14, 2011

I think the EPA has gotten completely out of control for a very simple reason. It is a tool in the hands of the president to crush the private enterprise system, to crush our ability to have energy, whether it's oil, gas, coal, nuclear. There's a real effort on the part of some in the president's party that don't like the American enterprise system and are trying to find a way to do everything they can to impede the growth of our economy and our energy independence.

—Mike Huckabee Presidential Forum,
Fox News Channel, December 3, 2011

ETHANOL

I support the subsidy of ethanol. I believe ethanol is an important part of our energy solution for this country.

—Campaign event, Des Moines, Iowa, May 27, 2011

GASOLINE PRICES

Well, you get the prices down by convincing people who are investing in gasoline futures, so to speak, the speculators—you let them understand that America is going to be producing enough energy for our needs. And that means we're going to start drilling for oil. We're going to use our natural gas resources, which are now extraordinarily plentiful, given new technology. We're going to use our coal resources. Of course, we're going to pursue all the renewables, but you have to have oil and gas to power America's economy.

—*On the Record w/Greta Van Susteren,*
Fox News Channel, April 25, 2011

The reason you're seeing these high prices is because of the extraordinary growth in demand globally and the inability of this nation to create sufficient supply. It's a supply-and-demand imbalance, and if we're going to get prices down, we're going to have to finally address our sources of energy. Instead of trying to find a scapegoat, as I watched the president [say] the other day, "We're gonna investigate and see who's gouging," well, that's always a good thing to do; there's nothing wrong with finding out who the gougers are, but that's not the reason for gasoline prices at the level we're seeing. The reason for these prices is because we have not kept our supply in line with our demand.

—Remarks to news reporters,
Manchester, New Hampshire, April 29, 2011

GLOBAL WARMING

I believe the world is getting warmer, and I believe that humans have contributed to that. It's important for us to reduce our emissions of pollutants and greenhouse gases that may be significant contributors.

—Campaign event,
Manchester, New Hampshire, June 3, 2011

My view is that we don't know what's causing climate change on this planet. And the idea of spending trillions and trillions of dollars to try and reduce CO_2 emissions is not the right course for us.

—Campaign event,
Pittsburgh, Pennsylvania, October 27, 2011

GREEN JOBS

As for job creation, studies show that "green" jobs might actually hurt employment more than they help it. Green energy is capital-intensive and tends to displace labor. Indeed, the track record in Europe shows that new "green" jobs came at a steep cost. Spain's experience, for example, reveals that each new "green" job created destroyed 2.2 others. The price tag in subsidies was exorbitant, rising to nearly $1.5 million per job in the wind industry. Even steeper job loss ratios can be found in the United Kingdom, where 3.7 jobs were lost for every new "green" job created. Here in the United States, despite the Obama administration's wishes, the marketplace is simply not absorbing green-collar workers. Of 3,586 recent graduates of a Department of Labor–sponsored "green" jobs training program, only 466 were able to find jobs. Taxpayer money spent on "green" training, it seems, was wasted.

—*Believe in America: Mitt Romney's Plan for*
Jobs and Economic Growth, 2011

[S]tudies of Europe's green job experiments have found that each new green job destroys several other jobs elsewhere in the economy.

—*Orange County Register*, October 24, 2011

NATURAL GAS

Natural gas is an energy source everyone can love. It is abundant domestically, it can substitute for oil in a number of applications, and it emits very little greenhouse gas. . . . America should be building gas pipelines as quickly as possible.

—*No Apology*, by Mitt Romney, 2010

NUCLEAR POWER

Nuclear power is a win-win; it's a domestic energy source with *zero* greenhouse gas emissions. The McKinsey analysis determined that nuclear power poses the single largest opportunity to reduce global greenhouse gas emissions. Without increased nuclear generation, the same study predicts global temperatures cannot achieve the two-degree Celsius goal. So, if you're serious about global warming, you have to say yes to nuclear, and if, like me, you're serious about energy security, you get to the same place.

I confess that I don't understand why some environmental activists still consider nuclear power such a boogeyman. They should consider the contemporary evidence—the United States now has 104 trouble-free nuclear reactors at sixty-five power plants. France gets 80 percent of its electrical power from nuclear generations. Nations all over the world are currently building new plants, and scores of naval vessels have been safely and efficiently running on nuclear power for decades. Vermont, the state which many consider to be the "greenest" in the country, gets 73 percent of its power from nuclear power. Nuclear generation has a safe and economic track record, and it is here to stay.

—*No Apology,* by Mitt Romney, 2010

OIL

[A] Romney administration will permit drilling wherever it can be done safely, taking into account local concerns. This includes the Gulf of Mexico, both the Atlantic and Pacific Outer Continental Shelves, Western lands, the Arctic National Wildlife Refuge, and off the Alaska coast. And it includes not only conventional reserves, but more recently discovered shale oil deposits as well. . . . Expanding energy production on this scale would bring lower prices, greater reliability of supply, and jobs, jobs, and jobs.

—Believe in America: Mitt Romney's Plan for
Jobs and Economic Growth, 2011

OIL REFINERIES

Secondly, with regards to big oil, big oil is making a lot of money right now. And I'd like to see them using that money to invest in refineries. Don't forget that when companies earn profit, that money's supposed to be reinvested in growth. And our refineries are old.

—GOP presidential debate,
Manchester, New Hampshire, June 5, 2007

TRANSPORTATION

One of the things you have to do is prioritize those things which are most important to you, and infrastructure and having good roads and bridges and rail lines and so forth and air traffic lines are essential for a strong economy. I'm willing to invest in those things and even borrow in circumstances where there's going to be a revenue stream that pays it back.

—Campaign event,
Hudson, New Hampshire, December 11, 2011

4

FOREIGN AFFAIRS
AND MILITARY

AFGHANISTAN

I want those troops to come home based upon not politics, not based upon economics, but instead based upon the conditions on the ground determined by the generals. But I also think we've learned that our troops shouldn't go off and try and fight a war of independence for another nation. Only the Afghanis can win Afghanistan's independence from the Taliban.

—GOP presidential debate,
Manchester, New Hampshire, June 13, 2011

Sometime within the next two years, we are going to draw down our troop strength and reach a point where the Afghan military is able to preserve the sovereignty of their own nation from the tyranny of the Taliban. That has to happen. It's time for the troops of Afghanistan to take on that responsibility according to, as I said in that last debate, according to the timetable established and communicated by the generals in the field.

—GOP presidential debate,
Ames, Iowa, August 11, 2011

AMERICA'S CHALLENGES

We face jihadism, the emergence of Asia as a competitor, our overspending, our overuse of oil, the failure of our health-care system. And yet we can't be burdened down with that. We have to recognize that what we have, as Americans, is the envy of the world. We have technology. We have innovation. We have great schools. We have great families. We have great homes. What we need to have is leadership that will tell us the truth, lay out the vision of where we can go, and actually lead. And I want to be able to do that for America.

—GOP presidential debate,
Dearborn, Michigan, October 9, 2007

CHINA

China can be a partner for world stability. There is no reason to think of China as we should of the Soviet Union that wishes to bury us. China wants to see us be a successful thriving economy. And they're, of course, building their military might. They will continue to build their military strength. They want to protect their oil flow. But, obviously, any nation that has a military is a nation we're going to have to watch very carefully. But China does not have to become a Soviet Union–type enemy, but instead can become—and increasingly has become—a trading partner with convergent interests.

—*National Journal*, February 10, 2007

China is acting like Adam Smith on steroids, buying oil from the world's worst and selling nuclear technology.

—Republican National Convention,
St. Paul, Minnesota, September 3, 2008

Chinese free enterprise is not like that of the West, at least not yet. Major industries continue to be state-owned and -operated. And absent from the Chinese system is the rule of law and regulation that shapes free enterprise elsewhere. It has failed to prevent widespread practices that have tainted products from dog food to infant formula, and it quite clearly welcomes the rampant theft of intellectual property from Western businesses. It is free enterprise on steroids—anything goes. China brazenly sells sensitive technologies to Iran and buys oil from genocidal Sudan, and it vigorously defends these nations against international sanction.

—*No Apology*, by Mitt Romney, 2010

"DON'T ASK, DON'T TELL"

No, actually when I first heard of the "Don't ask, don't tell" policy, I thought it sounded awfully silly and didn't think that'd be very effective, and I turned out to be wrong. It's been the policy now in the military for, what, ten, fifteen years? And it seems to be working. And I agree with what Mayor Giuliani said, that this is not the time to put in place a major change, a social experiment, in the middle of a war going on. I wouldn't change it at this point. We can look at it down the road. But it does seem to me that we have much bigger issues as a nation that we ought to be talking about than that policy right now.

—GOP presidential debate,
Manchester, New Hampshire, June 5, 2007

GROWING THE MILITARY

Well, I'm recommending that we add 100,000 active-duty personnel to our military. We're right now at about 1.5 million. Take that up to about 1.6 million. We found in our state that we were losing enrollees for the National Guard at about 6 percent per year. And the legislature and I got together and passed something called the Welcome Home Bill. We said, you know what, if you'll sign up for the National Guard, we'll pay for your entire education for four years. We put in some other benefits as well—life insurance and other features that we decided to pay for. And the result of that was, the next year enrollments went up 30 percent. And so if we want more people to sign up for the military, we have to improve the deal. And frankly, our GI Bill has gotten a little old. We need to update our funding level for that, so that young people who go into the military get a full ride as they come home and get to go into college.

—GOP presidential debate,
Boca Raton, Florida, January 24, 2008

GUANTANAMO BAY

Some people have said, we ought to close Guantanamo. My view is, we ought to double Guantanamo.

—GOP presidential debate,
Columbia, South Carolina, May 15, 2007

My views as expressed during the campaign is that Gitmo plays an important role, that it should be kept open, that bringing those terrorists to our soil would pose a potential threat in terms of their interactions with prisoners here. As we know, sending them back to other countries, in some cases, has led to their being on the battlefield and killing American servicemen and women. There is a real cost to closing a facility which is able to house those that have been taken in conflict. Treating terrorists as if they're common criminals entitled to legal representation if they cannot furnish them at their own expense is a remarkable breach of wartime philosophy.

—*Human Events*, September 28, 2009

INTERROGATION TECHNIQUES

I don't think you're going to find people—and I think it's wise—
defining exactly what the line is in torture, because I don't think
you want the enemy combatants to know what you're planning on doing. I don't think you want them to know, "Oh, this is
what they're going to do, they can't do more than this." I think
you want to leave it somewhat unclear.

—Republican Jewish Coalition Victory 2008 Forum,
Washington, D.C., October 16, 2007

IRAN

I think it's unacceptable for Iran to have a nuclear weapon. Unacceptable to our interests and to the interest of the civilized world. For that reason I think we should exert every source of our world pressure to keep Iran from pursuing that course. And, of course, the military option must be left on the table.

—*RealClearPolitics*, February 23, 2007

The Iranian leadership is the greatest immediate threat to the world since the fall of the Soviet Union, and before that, Nazi Germany.

—*Human Events*, October 22, 2009

The Iranian regime threatens not only Israel, but also every other nation in the region, and ultimately the world. It is a repressive regime . . . an intractable enemy of liberty and human rights . . . the world's leading sponsor of terrorism and subversive war. The threat it poses to the world would take on an entirely new dimension if Iran were allowed to become a nuclear power.

—*Human Events*, October 22, 2009

And with regards to Iran, which perhaps represents the greatest existential threat to Israel, we have to make it abundantly clear: It is unacceptable—and I take that word carefully—it is unacceptable for Iran to become a nuclear nation.

—GOP presidential debate,
Orlando, Florida, September 22, 2011

IRAQ

It was the right decision to go into Iraq. I supported it at the time; I support it now. It was not well managed in the—after the takedown of Saddam Hussein and his military. That was done brilliantly, an extraordinary success. But in the years that followed, it was not well—we were undermanaged, underprepared, underplanned, understaffed, and then we come into the phase that we have now. The plan that President Bush and General Petraeus put together is working. It's changing lives there. And perhaps most importantly, it's making sure that Al Qaeda and no other group like them is becoming a superpower, if you will, in the communities, and having a safe haven from which they launch attacks against us. It's critical for us. When we think about debating the Democrats, they might want to go back and talk about what happened at the beginning. But the most important issue is what do we do now, and their just run and retreat regardless of the consequences is going to be a real problem for them when they face a debate with a Republican on the stage.

—GOP presidential debate,
Boca Raton, Florida, January 24, 2008

ISRAEL

President Obama has thrown Israel under the bus. He has disrespected Israel and undermined its ability to negotiate peace. He has also violated a first principle of American foreign policy, which is to stand firm by our friends.

—Press release, May 18, 2011

I want every country in the region that harbors aggressive designs against Israel to understand that their ambition is futile. And that pursuing it will cost them very dearly.

—Republican Jewish Coalition Presidential Candidates Forum, Washington, D.C., December 7, 2011

JIHADISM

Recognize to win the war on jihad, we have to not only have a strong military of our own—and we need a stronger military—we also need to have strong friends around the world and help moderate Muslims reject the extreme. Because ultimately the only people who can finally defeat these radical Islamic jihadists are the Muslims themselves.

—GOP presidential debate, Des Moines, Iowa, August 5, 2007

The real problem is that jihadists want to conquer the world. They want to eradicate a Jewish state and the Jewish people.

—Republican Jewish Coalition Victory 2008 Forum,
Washington, D.C., October 16, 2007

And finally, let's consider the greatest challenge facing America, and for that matter facing the entire civilized world: the threat of radical, violent jihad. As you know, in one wing of the world of Islam there's a conviction that all governments should be destroyed and replaced by a religious caliphate. These jihadists will battle any form of democracy because to them democracy is blasphemous, because it says that citizens, not God, shape the law. They find the idea of human equality to be equally offensive. They hate everything we believe about freedom just as we hate everything they believe about radical jihad. To battle this threat, we've sent the most courageous and brave soldiers in the world.

—Conservative Political Action Conference,
Washington, D.C., February 7, 2008

LIBYA

Well, first, I support military action in Libya. I support our troops there and the mission that they've been given.

—*The Hugh Hewitt Show*, March 21, 2011

The world is about to be rid of Muammar el-Qaddafi, the brutal tyrant who terrorized the Libyan people. It is my hope that Libya will now move toward a representative form of government that supports freedom, human rights, and the rule of law. As a first step, I call on this new government to arrest and extradite the mastermind behind the bombing of Pan Am 103, Abdelbaset Mohmed Ali al-Megrahi, so justice can finally be done.

—Press release, August 22, 2011

MAHMOUD AHMADINEJAD

Iranian President Mahmoud Ahmadinejad has gone well beyond the boundary of outrage—beginning with his calculated desecration of history. When he denies the Holocaust, he could care less about history. His point is about the present and the future. His purpose is not merely to deny the Holocaust, but also to deny Israel. He is testing the waters. He wants to know who will object. And how they will register their objection.

—*Human Events*, October 22, 2009

I would not meet with Mahmoud Ahmadinejad. He should be excluded from diplomatic society. In fact, he should be indicted for the crime of incitement to genocide under Article III of the Genocide Convention.

—Republican Jewish Coalition Presidential Candidates Forum, Washington, D.C., December 7, 2011

New START

New START is a major victory for Russia. One treaty observer, having completed a line-by-line analysis of the agreement, concluded that every single provision favors Russia or is neutral; not one favors the United States. Like most Americans, I believe that the world would be safer if there were no weapons of mass destruction. But I also believe that the world is safer if America is strong. In fact, the stronger we are relative to nations like Russia, the safer the world is. I also believe that missile defense is an urgent priority that we must not allow to be restricted. New START, as currently drafted, should not be approved by the Senate.

—*National Review*, July 26, 2010

NORTH KOREA

North Korea is in contempt of the world and the United States. On the very day the president gives a speech about nuclear nonproliferation, North Korea carries out a missile test. And then on our Memorial Day, they carried out an underground nuclear explosion. They're making it very clear that they're thumbing their nose at the world. And with a rogue nation like that, you have to be very aggressive in defending ourselves with missile defense.

—*Fox News Sunday* with Chris Wallace,
Fox News Channel, May 31, 2009

OSAMA BIN LADEN

This is a global effort we're going to have to lead to overcome this jihadist effort. It's more than Osama bin Laden. But he is going to pay, and he will die.

—GOP presidential debate,
Simi Valley, California, May 3, 2007

I think the killing of Osama bin Laden is an enormous success, and I don't know if it helps or hurts the president politically, but I really don't care. The right thing is we got the bad guy, and the nation celebrates that. We're all Americans. This is not a Republican or a Democrat thing; this is an American thing.

—Remarks to news reporters,
New Hampshire, May 3, 2011

To win this fight for America's future, we will have to rise above politics. When members of SEAL Team Six boarded their helicopters, they did so not as Republicans or Democrats or independents, they did so as Americans. And the final image that Osama bin Laden took with him straight to hell was not a party symbol—not a Republican elephant or a Democratic donkey—but an American flag on the shoulder of one straight-shooting U.S. Navy SEAL.

—Veterans of Foreign Wars National Convention,
San Antonio, Texas, August 30, 2011

RUSSIA

Russia and the oil states are siphoning more than $500 billion a year from us in what could become the greatest transfer of economic wealth in the history of the world.

—Republican National Convention,
St. Paul, Minnesota, September 3, 2008

SPENDING

In the face of evil and radical jihad, and given the inevitable military ambitions of China, we must act to rebuild our military might, raise military spending to 4 percent of our GDP, purchase the most modern armament, reshape our fighting forces for the asymmetric demands we now face, and give the veterans the care they deserve.

—Conservative Political Action Conference,
Washington, D.C., February 7, 2008

SYRIA

It has taken President Obama far too long to speak out force-fully against Assad and his vicious crackdown in Syria. In the early stages of this crisis, the Obama Administration referred to Assad as a "reformer," which had the effect of emboldening Assad and discouraging the dissidents. America must show leadership on the world stage and work to move these developing nations toward modernity. This means using the bullhorn of the presidency and not remaining silent for too long while voices of freedom and dissent are under attack.

—Press release, August 18, 2011

TALIBAN

The Taliban harbored the terrorists who killed 3,000 Americans on September 11th. The Taliban continues to wage war against us and our allies, a conflict in which we have lost over 1,800 troops. The Taliban receives arms and training from Iran. And the Taliban seeks to reinstate a tyrannical government that violently rejects basic notions of human rights and oppresses minorities. The Taliban is clearly a bitter enemy of the United States.

—Press release, December 19, 2011

VETERANS

After declaring a "Hire a Veteran" month in November in Massachusetts while governor: Our veterans know the meaning of service better than anyone else, and they aren't about to quit working when they come home. The best reward we can provide our vets for their service isn't a medal or a check—it's a livelihood and a means of supporting themselves and their families.

—Press release, November 3, 2005

WIRETAPPING

Noting that he would not do so without a judge's approval: And if it means we have to go into a mosque to wiretap or a church, then that's exactly where we're going to go because we're going to do whatever it takes to protect the American people. And I hear from time to time people say, hey, wait a second, we have civil liberties we have to worry about. But don't forget the most important civil liberty I expect from my government is my right to be kept alive, and that's what we're going to have to do.

—GOP presidential debate,
Durham, New Hampshire, September 5, 2007

5

GOVERNMENT AND POLITICS

AL GORE

It's good to be back home in Mackinac [Michigan]. One of the things I like best is that there are no cars on the island. Unfortunately, that's Al Gore's vision for all of America.

—Mackinac Republican Leadership Conference,
September 22, 2007

And I have one more recommendation for energy conservation: Let's keep Al Gore's private jet on the ground.

—Republican National Convention,
St. Paul, Minnesota, September 3, 2008

AMERICA

On being asked, during a debate at the Ronald Reagan Presidential Library, "What do you dislike most about America?": Gosh. I love America. I'm afraid I'm going to be at a loss for words because America for me is not just our rolling mountains and hills and streams and great cities. It's the American people. And the American people are the greatest people in the world. What makes America the greatest nation in the world is the heart of the American people: hardworking, innovative, risk-taking, God-loving, family-oriented American people. It's that optimism we thank Ronald Reagan for. Thank you, Mrs. Reagan, for opening up this place in his memory for us. It is that optimism about this great people that makes this the greatest nation on earth.

—GOP presidential debate,
Simi Valley, California, May 3, 2007

Our parents, our grandparents, gave us the greatest nation in the history of the earth. The values, the economic vitality, the military we enjoy keeps us safe and prosperous. What are we going to give our kids?

—West Virginia Delegate Convention, February 5, 2008

I'm convinced that unless America changes course, we could become the France of the twenty-first century. Still a great nation, but not the leader of the world, not the superpower. And to me that's unthinkable.

—Conservative Political Action Conference,
Washington, D.C., February 7, 2008

In a world where others have lost their liberty by trading it away for the false promises of the state, we choose to hold to our founding values. We'll stop these power-seekers where they stand. We will preserve America's character as the land of liberty. We welcome those who seek and will defend freedom. We admire the entrepreneur, the inventor, the innovator. We will insist on greatness from every one of our citizens, and rather than apologizing for who we are or for what we've accomplished, we'll celebrate our nation's strength and its goodness. American patriots have defeated tyrants, liberated the oppressed, rescued the afflicted. America's model of innovation, capitalism, free enterprise has lifted literally billions of the world's poor out of poverty. America has been a force for good like no other in the world, and for that, we will make no apology.

—Values Voter Summit,
Washington, D.C., September 17, 2010

I refuse to believe that America is just another place on the map with a flag. I believe that America is an exceptional nation, of freedom and opportunity and hope. We *are* an exceptional land! The America that you and I believe in has a goodness and a greatness that creates a unique American genius. And that genius has blessed the world, led the world, even saved the world from the unimaginable darkness that could have occurred.

—Conservative Political Action Conference,
Washington, D.C., February 11, 2011

We are a people who, in the language of our Declaration of Independence, hold certain truths to be self-evident: namely, that all men are endowed by their Creator with certain unalienable rights. It is our belief in the universality of these unalienable rights that leads us to our exceptional role on the world stage, that of a great champion of human dignity and human freedom.

—The Citadel,
Charleston, South Carolina, October 7, 2011

God did not create this country to be a nation of followers. America is not destined to be one of several equally balanced global powers. America must lead the world, or someone else will. Without American leadership, without clarity of American purpose and resolve, the world becomes a far more dangerous place, and liberty and prosperity would surely be among the first casualties.

—The Citadel, Charleston, South Carolina, October 7, 2011

BARACK OBAMA

He should forget entirely about reelection and focus solely on helping the nation at a critical time. He should dismiss the people who helped him win the election and bring in people who are above politics and above party. He should surround himself with statesmen and economists, businesspeople and leaders. In some ways it would be beneficial if our presidency consisted of only one term. That way the President would think about his legacy and the future of the country rather than reelection and partisanship.

—*CNNMoney/Fortune*, November 7, 2008

I know that people recognize that this is a man who is a decent fellow. He's intelligent. He's well intentioned. He's just not experienced in the matters that we're dealing with right now. And, you know, I hope he's able to get this economy turned around.

—*Larry King Live*, CNN, March 19, 2009

This is a president who is learning on the fly. He's never turned anything around before. He hasn't had the experience of leading a nation or a business or a state in trouble. And the first rule I can tell him is focus, focus, focus. Focus on the job at hand, getting this economy going, and making sure there are no errors, no mistakes, no excessive spending. It's too risky, given the fact that the economy is hanging by a thread.

—*Larry King Live*, CNN, March 19, 2009

We have a president who added trillions of dollars to federal spending. We just put almost $800 billion into a stimulus plan.

Not one dollar of that is going to modernize our military. It is a course which I find very difficult to understand.

—*Fox News Sunday* with Chris Wallace,
Fox News Channel, May 31, 2009

Like other presidents before him, Barack Obama inherited a recession. But unlike them, he has made it worse, not better.

—*USA Today*, December 2, 2009

And the president has felt so giddy that he fit in forty rounds of golf. Mind you, I think the country's probably better off when he's listening to advice from his caddy rather than from his economic advisers.

—Values Voter Summit,
Washington, D.C., September 17, 2010

Isn't it ironic that a president who said he would unite the country has turned out to be the most divisive in history? But he has succeeded in one way. He has united virtually all of America against him.

—Values Voter Summit,
Washington, D.C., September 17, 2010

President Obama has stood watch over the greatest job loss in modern American history. And that, my friends, is one inconvenient truth that will haunt this president throughout history.

—Conservative Political Action Conference,
Washington, D.C., February 11, 2011

I think the citizenship test has been passed. I believe the president was born in the United States.

—*The Kudlow Report*, CNBC,
April 12, 2011

I don't think he really loves free enterprise and capitalism. I think he has disdain for the free markets. I think he has disdain for the states.

—Public conference call, Las Vegas, Nevada, May 16, 2011

Barack Obama has failed America.

—Presidential announcement speech,
Stratham, New Hampshire, June 2, 2011

Look, he's a nice guy. He's well-spoken. He can talk a dog off a meat wagon, and yet he hasn't delivered.

—Campaign event,
Manchester, New Hampshire, June 3, 2011

Referring to Barack Obama referencing RomneyCare as an inspiration for ObamaCare: Well, the great news is that when I finally debate President Obama, it will be wonderful, because he won't be able to say I'm some heartless Republican that doesn't care about people. He'll say I was the inspiration for what he did. And I'll say, "Mr. President, how come you didn't call? How come you didn't ask me about your plan, because it will not work."

—*Piers Morgan Tonight*, CNN, June 6, 2011

When you see what this president has done to the economy in 3 years, you know why America doesn't want to find out what he can do in 8.

—Twitter: @MittRomney, August 5, 2011

Now, I'm asked now and then, "Why isn't Obama working? Why is the Obama economy so tepid? How has it failed so badly to put Americans to work?" He'll be giving a speech in a couple of days. I know what's coming. I haven't read it, but I know it's coming. I've seen version one, two, three, four, and five. They're not working. And the reason is, you know what? I mentioned a moment ago that we're now using smartphones, not pay phones. President Obama's strategy is a pay phone strategy and we're in a smartphone world. And so we're going to have to change. What he's doing is taking quarters and stuffing them into the pay phone and thinking—can't figure out why she's not working. It's not connected anymore, Mr. President. All right? Your pay phone strategy doesn't work in a smartphone world. I mean, we're going to hear about another stimulus and more quarters, trillions of them, getting stuffed in that pay phone and I know what the results will be. They won't be getting America back to work.

—Campaign event,
North Las Vegas, Nevada, September 6, 2011

BEN BERNANKE

On being asked if Bernanke would be in a Romney administration: No, I'd be looking for somebody new. I think Ben Bernanke has overinflated the amount of currency that he's created. QE2 [second round of central bank policy to stimulate economy] did not work. It did not get Americans back to work. It did not get the economy going again. We're still seeing declining numbers in prior quarter estimates as to what the growth would be. We're growing now at 1 percent to 1.5 percent. The plan I put forward just two days ago in Nevada will grow our economy at 4 percent per year for four years and add—add—11.5 million jobs. That's a very different approach than Ben Bernanke's taken, and it's a demonstrably different approach than Barack Obama has taken, and that's in part because we have very different life experiences.

—GOP presidential debate,
Simi Valley, California, September 7, 2011

DEMOCRATIC PARTY

We are the party of the revolutionaries; they [Democrats] are
the party of the monarchists.

—Republican Party event in
northern Virginia, May 2, 2009

DEPENDENCY

I felt very strongly that the social programs of the sixties and seventies, the liberal agenda—I'll call it the Johnson agenda—had hurt working families, had hurt the poor in many instances. And while the liberals had the best of intentions, I felt that the programs themselves had created a permanent underclass and had fostered poverty instead of eliminating it.

—*The Atlantic*, September 2005

The threat to our culture comes from within. In the 1960s, there were welfare programs that created a culture of poverty in our country. Now, some people think we won that battle when we reformed welfare. But the liberals haven't given up. At every turn, they tried to substitute government largesse for individual responsibility. They fight to strip work requirements from welfare, to put more people on Medicaid, and remove more and more people from having to pay any income tax whatsoever. Dependency is death to initiative, risk-taking, and opportunity. Dependency is culture killing. It's a drug. We've got to fight it like the poison it is.

—Conservative Political Action Conference,
Washington, D.C., February 7, 2008

If the government is willing to give away money, there will always be a long line to get it.

—*No Apology*, by Mitt Romney, 2010

ENTITLEMENT SOCIETY

And in an entitlement society everyone receives about the same rewards regardless of the education they pursue, regardless of their effort, regardless of the willingness that they have to take risk. And that which is earned by some is redistributed to others. And in that kind of setting, by the way, the only people who get truly disproportionate rewards are the people who do the redistributing—the government folks. Entitlement societies are, of course, praised in academic circles where they're far removed from the reality of a competitive world. You see they replace opportunity with certainty. Certainty that everyone in the entitlement society will enjoy nearly the same rewards. But there's another certainty. They'll all be poor. Because in an entitlement society the invigorating pursuit of happiness is replaced by the deadening reality that there's no prospect of a better tomorrow. Risk-taking disappears. Innovation disappears. Small businesses disappear, and they're replaced by a large government bureaucracy and government enterprises.

—Republican Jewish Coalition Presidential Candidates Forum,
Washington, D.C., December 7, 2011

GEORGE W. BUSH

I'm not a historian, and we haven't got enough time and distance to assess that. But I think that it will be seen as successes and accomplishments where he gets good grades, and places where he will not get good grades. And clearly, as I've pointed out, with regards to the post-Saddam-collapse management of the Iraq conflict, he will not get good grades there. I think on education and No Child Left Behind, he'll get a good grade. I think [he'll get a good grade on] rebuilding the economy, pulling us out of what could have been a very severe recession or worse following 9/11 and the collapse of the Internet bubble. We were already headed down. We were in the normal, cyclical downturn when the president came in. We could have really gone into a tailspin and he was able to help pull us back. And he brought dignity and personal integrity back to the White House after a very unfortunate series of events during the Clinton years.

—*Newsweek*, October 8, 2007

Regardless of his other mistakes, that man made it very clear that he was going to defend America. And that it was his number one priority. And he did it with every ounce of his energy. And for that I respect him, and think he deserves credit.

—*Your World with Neil Cavuto*,
Fox News Channel, March 3, 2010

HECKLERS

The way this is going to work is that you get to ask your question, I get to give my answer. If you don't like my answer, you can vote for someone else.

—Iowa State Fair, Des Moines, Iowa, August 11, 2011

INCENTIVES

I remember, I was looking at the budget in our state. There was a line in there for homeless shelters. And I said, "What's this sub-account here for hotels under homeless shelters." They said, "Oh, Governor, you have to understand, if someone comes to a homeless shelter and we're full, we tell them go to a hotel and we'll pick up the bill." I said, "I bet the word gets around, you know." So I changed the incentive. I told them immediately put in place this new rule. Which [is] if someone comes to a homeless shelter, and it's full, you tell them you'll make room. And the person who's been there the longest—three, four, five months—they get to go to the hotel. Now before that change in incentive went in place, guess how many rooms a night we were renting in Massachusetts? Five hundred and ninety-nine rooms a night on average. In the tens of millions of dollars of cost. After we changed that incentive, you know how many rooms we rent a night? Zero. Zero. Incentives make a difference.

> —Conservative Political Action Conference Florida,
> Orlando, Florida, September 23, 2011

INEFFICIENCY

Government inefficiency wastes resources and places a burden on citizens and employers that's harmful to our future. And anytime I see waste, or patronage, it bothers me.

—*The Atlantic*, September 2005

JOHN McCAIN

John McCain said he thinks about being president every day in the shower. I guess I will turn to the words of *Star Wars:* It's in a galaxy far, far away.

—News conference,
Boston, Massachusetts, December 14, 2005

Well, obviously, having the support of Senator McCain means a great deal to me nationally, but particularly here in New Hampshire, where Senator McCain is beloved by so many people, where this evening, we just had a town meeting, this was the very place that Senator McCain announced his candidacy in the past. So, old roots, old connections, and the association with someone who is an unquestioned hero and patriot is something which I value personally and of course, I think it's a good statement politically that we are coming together as a party to get behind folks we believe in.

—*Hannity*, Fox News Channel, January 4, 2012

LIBERALS

I went to a memorial service relating to the 9/11 tragedy and the minister who stood up, got up, and said that it was time for us to focus on the root causes of terrorism, lack of good housing and lack of good health care. It's just extraordinary what you hear in the liberal world.

—Republican Jewish Coalition Victory 2008 Forum,
Washington, D.C., October 16, 2007

You see, liberals would replace opportunity with dependency on government largesse. They grow government and raise taxes to put more people on Medicaid, to take work requirements out of welfare, and to grow the ranks of those who pay no taxes at all. Dependency is death to initiative, to risk-taking and opportunity. It's time to stop the spread of government dependency and fight it like the poison it is. You know, it's time for the party of big ideas, not the party of Big Brother.

—Republican National Convention,
St. Paul, Minnesota, September 3, 2008

Course, it wasn't so long ago, don't forget, that they were flying high. Remember the commentators' legs at MSNBC were tingling. *Time* magazine's cover declared that the Republican elephant was an endangered species.

—Values Voter Summit,
Washington, D.C., September 17, 2010

LIMITED GOVERNMENT

The idea of government running anything and thinking it will do a better job than the private sector is a very bad idea indeed, and suggests a lack of understanding of how our economy works.

—*The Kudlow Report*, CNBC, February 7, 2007

We know the source of America's strength. It's the citizens of this country, and all that free people can achieve. Free, hardworking, family-oriented, risk-taking, opportunity-seeking, patriotic American people have always been the source of this nation's strength, and they always will be. And here in Washington, the best policies are those policies that expand the freedoms of individuals, that broaden their opportunities, that allow individuals to keep more of what they earn, that afford them better education, that let them choose their own health care, and that turn loose the free enterprise system so that it can create jobs.

—Values Voter Summit,
Washington, D.C., September 19, 2009

But I think we all agree that government has a legitimate role in defending the country, managing our justice system, and overseeing our schools, or some portion of our schools. But I agree with many across this country that government has gone way, way, way too far. And that rather than protecting the free enterprise system and individual freedom, it is smothering the free enterprise system, and smothering the innovative pioneering spirit that's America.

—*Your World with Neil Cavuto*,
Fox News Channel, March 3, 2010

NANCY PELOSI

Referring to the Republican Party gaining control of the United States House of Representatives and Nancy Pelosi losing her role as Speaker of the House: We Republicans are flying high because Nancy Pelosi is flying coach.

—Republican Jewish Coalition, Las Vegas, Nevada, April 2, 2011

POLITICAL CAMPAIGNS

Referring to helping his mother, Lenore, win the Republican primary nomination for Senate in 1970: I drove a minivan to all 83 counties in Michigan. I learned about campaigning and what I learned is that there is no substitute for retail face-to-face campaigning.

—Campaigns & Elections, August 2007

PUBLIC LIFE

The world of politics is turbulent and changing and dynamic. Public life has extraordinary rewards. It also is a very mercurial setting. A slip of the tongue or a misstatement can lead to a significant reversal.

—*Boston Globe*, March 4, 2005

Referring to his father's comment in 1967 that he had been "brainwashed" by U.S. officials during a trip to Vietnam two years earlier, words that are partially credited for harming George Romney's campaign for the 1968 Republican presidential nomination: It did tell me you have to be very, very careful in your choice of words. The careful selection of words is something I'm more attuned to because Dad fell into that quagmire.

—*The Atlantic*, September 2005

You've got to be really careful about what you say and do anywhere you are. I actually had a dream about being in [a] parking garage and having somebody in front of me taking too long to get their change and honking the horn and then yelling back, and getting out and yelling at each other and then seeing it on YouTube the next day. So I said "OK," I've got to really be careful, you know, in my personal life.

—*RealClearPolitics*, February 23, 2007

REFORM

The key thing you have to consider, as you look at what's happening in the federal government, is that Washington is broken. We need to have fundamental change in the way business in Washington is carried out. What that means is we're going to have to have leadership that can reorganize the government. We're going to have about 40 percent of the government employees turn over in the next couple of terms. And if we can reduce the employment there, [what is] more important is to go through all the agencies, all the departments, all the programs and cut out the unnecessary and the wasteful.

—GOP presidential debate,
Columbia, South Carolina, May 15, 2007

We have, in the federal government, 342 different economic development programs, often administered by different departments. We don't need 342. We probably don't need a hundred of those. We probably need a lot fewer than that. We have forty different programs for workforce training. There are probably five or six that are really working and a lot that are not working terribly well. We can get rid of some of those. We have thirteen different programs to prevent teenage pregnancy. Well, they're obviously not working real well, and we can probably cut it down to one or two that are making a difference. And so what anyone in the private sector's learned how to do is to focus their resources on those things that have the biggest impact, that are most important. Surely, protecting our country and our defense of our military is critical. Getting our free market finally able to allow all of our citizens to have insurance, health insurance, that's something we did in Massachusetts. Improving

151

our schools with school choice, better pay for better teachers—
these are a lot of things that we can do, but they don't require
us to eliminate the things that are most critical in our society.
Instead they require us to get rid of those things that are unnecessary. And the sacrifice we need from the American people, it's
this: It's saying let the programs that don't work go.

—GOP presidential debate,
Johnston, Iowa, December 12, 2007

And Washington needs fundamental, top-to-bottom change.
We're not going to have somebody inside Washington turn
Washington inside out, just not going to happen. We're going to
have to change our spending habits and our taxing habits. We're
going to have to finally find a way to get ourselves energy independent and energy secure. We're going to have to fix education
in this country. We need to get health care for all of our citizens;
free-market health care, not government health care. We've
been talking about these things for decades and decades. And
yet, somehow, just sending the same people to Washington, but
in different chairs, is not going to result in a different outcome.
And that's why when people of this country have looked at the
change that we need in Washington, they say, "Let's bring someone in from the outside and make that change." And I think
it has to be somebody who's had executive leadership, who's
brought change.

—GOP presidential debate,
Milford, New Hampshire, January 6, 2008

REGULATION

Look, no free market can work in the absence of laws and regulation. What Republicans need to do—and I'm one of those that probably falls prey to this now and then—is not just give the short answer, but to say, look, we're not against all regulation, we're against all regulation that's unnecessary, bloated, overwhelming, burdensome. We want to get regulations up to date and streamlined.

—*Larry King Live*, CNN, March 23, 2010

REPUBLICAN PARTY

We're the party of opportunity. We're the party of keeping taxes down. We're the party that want people to have choice in their schools and choice in their health care.

—*This Week* with George Stephanopoulos,
ABC News, June 14, 2009

Of course the president accuses us of being the party of no. It's as if he thinks that by saying no, it's by definition a bad thing. In fact, as you know, it's right and praiseworthy to say no to bad things. It's right to say no to cap and trade, no to card check, no to government health care, no to higher taxes. My party, our party, can never be a rubber stamp for rubber-check spending. But before we move away from this no epithet that the Democrats are fond of trying to apply to us, let's ask the Obama folks why they say no: no to a balanced budget, no to reforming entitlements, no to malpractice reform, no to missile defense in Eastern Europe, no to prosecuting Khalid Sheikh Mohammed and a military tribunal—no to tax cuts that create jobs. You see, we conservatives don't have a corner on saying no. We're just the ones who say it when it's the right thing to say.

—Conservative Political Action Conference,
Washington, D.C., February 18, 2010

Ours is the party of opportunity, and theirs is the party of handout.

—Republican Jewish Coalition,
Las Vegas, Nevada, April 2, 2011

RONALD REAGAN

The older I get, the smarter Ronald Reagan gets.
—*This Week* with George Stephanopoulos, ABC News, February 18, 2007

Ronald Reagan was a president of strength. His philosophy was a philosophy of strength: a strong military, a strong economy, and strong families.
—GOP presidential debate, Simi Valley, California, May 3, 2007

As years go on, Ronald Reagan gets smarter and smarter. And I recognize in him a great leader who had a great deal of wisdom as it dealt with the challenges of his day. And I believe America is not going to follow the path of Hillary Clinton or Barack Obama or John Edwards. I don't think we're going to take a sharp left turn—big government, big taxes, Big Brother. I believe, instead, that we're going to pursue the course Ronald Reagan outlined of strength and goodness—strength and goodness in our homes, the strength of a vibrant economy, and the strength of a strong military.
—Campaign event, Spartanburg, South Carolina, December 18, 2007

Here at home, Reagan saw a federal government that had become, like a diseased heart, enlarged and sclerotic. Paving a path trod today by the Tea Party, he sharply cut taxes to restore economic growth. He took painful measures to rein in double-digit inflation. He fought to cut federal spending. He sought to restore our Founding Fathers' vision of American greatness and limited government. Reagan's legacy is very much alive. Only amiable dunces cannot see that.
—*USA Today*, January 23, 2011

RUSH LIMBAUGH

He's a very powerful voice among conservatives. And I listen to him. A lot of other people listen to him. He's not a spokesman for the party, of course. But we don't have one spokesman right now. That's just one of the features of not having either House in Congress or having the White House. You don't have an official place to be heard.

—*Larry King Live*, CNN, March 19, 2009

SARAH PALIN

Boy, she was able to connect with our party in a very power-ful way, ignite a lot of enthusiasm and excitement. That kind of political skill is rare. I hadn't met her before the announce-ment that she was going to be our VP nominee. And I thought, boy, she's going to have a tough time up there on the stage at the Republican convention. Was I wrong. She got out there and just lit the place up, and was able to draw a lot of support from across the nation. She's a powerful voice.

—*Larry King Live*, CNN, March 19, 2009

Energetic, positive force in the Republican party, a leader in our party, and having a positive impact on bringing out a lot of folks that were in the silent majority are finding they're not silent anymore. That's a good thing.

—*Larry King Live*, CNN, March 23, 2010

STATES' RIGHTS

Referring to Barack Obama's historic health-care program, the Patient Protection and Affordable Care Act: Well, states have rights that the federal government doesn't have. Under the Tenth Amendment of the Constitution, the powers of the federal government are specifically limited. The states have the rights to, for instance, mandate kids going to school, mandate auto insurance. States have certain rights that they can exercise. We can try different things in different states, find out what works and what doesn't. But the last thing you want to see is the federal government usurping the power of states. This is a federalist nation. It's unconstitutional. By the way, it's, it's also bad policy.

—*Good Morning America*, ABC News, February 1, 2011

TEA PARTY

I think it shows a great deal of energy and passion on the part of the American people to say, Stop, we're going the wrong way, enough already, let's get things right in America. And America is headed in the wrong direction. This growing government, the increase in taxes, the more intrusiveness of government has made a lot of people very angry and they want to see change in Washington. They want to see the Washington politicians that have been voting for this kind of intrusive government thrown out of office. And I think it's a good thing. I think Washington politicians need to understand there's a lot of focus and energy around what's happening, and people aren't going to take it a lot longer.

—*On the Record w/Greta Van Susteren*,
Fox News Channel, January 8, 2010

Almost 2½ centuries after the original Boston Tea Party of 1773, the idea of limited government that inspired our forebears is very much alive. The growth of government is not some inexorable force. In a democracy, we the people decide. Thanks to the Tea Party, there's real hope that we can rein in our profligate federal government.

—*Orlando Sentinel*, April 14, 2011

I don't think you carry cards in the Tea Party. I believe in a lot of what the Tea Party believes in. The Tea Party believes that government's too big, taxing too much, and that we ought to get to the work of getting Americans to work. So I put together a plan with a whole series of points of how we can get

America's economy going again. Tea Party people like that. So if the Tea Party is for keeping government small and spending down, and helping us create jobs, then, hey, I'm for the Tea Party.

—GOP presidential debate,
Simi Valley, California, September 7, 2011

TED KENNEDY

Referring to his 1994 run for the U.S. Senate seat held by Kennedy:
A white, male, Mormon millionaire was not going to beat Ted
Kennedy in Massachusetts, but someone deserved to go out
there and give him a real run for his money.

—*60 Minutes*, CBS, May 13, 2007

You learn a lot in running a campaign. I don't imagine I could
have become governor of Massachusetts had I not first had the
learning experience of facing Ted Kennedy. He was a tough
schoolmaster.

—*U.S. News Digital Weekly*, June 12, 2009

The loss of Senator Ted Kennedy is a sad event for America, and
especially for Massachusetts. The last son of Rose Fitzgerald and
Joseph Kennedy was granted a much longer life than his broth-
ers, and he filled those years with endeavor and achievement
that would have made them proud.

In 1994, I joined the long list of those who ran against Ted
and came up short. But he was the kind of man you could like
even if he was your adversary. I came to admire Ted enormously
for his charm and sense of humor—qualities all the more im-
pressive in a man who had known so much loss and sorrow. I
will always remember his great personal kindness, and the fighting spirit he brought to every cause he served and every challenge he faced. I was proud to know Ted Kennedy as a friend,
and today my family and I mourn the passing of this big-
hearted, unforgettable man.

—Personal statement regarding Ted Kennedy's death, August 26, 2009

THE CLINTONS

Referring to Hillary Clinton running for president in the 2008 general election: Hillary Clinton wants to run the largest enterprise in the world, the government of the United States. It employs millions of people, trillions of dollars in revenue. She hasn't run a corner store. She hasn't run a state. She hasn't run a city. She has never run anything. And the idea that she could learn to be president, you know, as an internship just doesn't make any sense.

—GOP presidential debate,
Orlando, Florida, October 21, 2007

In response to being asked how he would run against Hillary Clinton with her husband, Bill, being her running mate for the 2008 general election: I frankly can't wait, because the idea of Bill Clinton back in the White House with nothing to do is something I just can't imagine.

—GOP presidential debate,
Boca Raton, Florida, January 24, 2008

I said before, Washington is broken. She is Washington to the core. She's been there too long. Bill Clinton's been there too long. The last thing America needs is sending the Clintons back to Washington.

—GOP presidential debate,
Boca Raton, Florida, January 24, 2008

THEODORE ROOSEVELT

I love Teddy Roosevelt. I read everything I can get my hands on about Teddy Roosevelt. Anybody who says "Bully" is a friend of mine. And his enthusiasm, his energy, his can-do attitude was just extraordinary.

—*RealClearPolitics*, February 23, 2007

I frankly don't know whether Teddy Roosevelt's policies would be accepted by the Republican party today, but Teddy Roosevelt was as Republican as any Republican I know.

—*RealClearPolitics*, February 23, 2007

WITHDRAWING FROM 2008 PRESIDENTIAL CAMPAIGN

Now, I disagree with Senator McCain on a number of issues, as you know. But I agree with him on doing whatever it takes to be successful in Iraq, and finding and executing Osama bin Laden. And I agree with him on eliminating Al Qaeda and terror worldwide. Now, if I fight on, in my campaign, all the way to the convention . . . I want you to know, I've given this a lot of thought—I'd forestall the launch of a national campaign and, frankly, I'd make it easier for Senator Clinton or Obama to win. Frankly, in this time of war, I simply cannot let my campaign be a part of aiding a surrender to terror. This isn't an easy decision. I hate to lose. My family, my friends, you, my supporters across the country, you've given a great deal to get me to where I have a shot to becoming president. If this were only about me, I'd go on. But it's never been only about me. I entered this race—I entered this race because I love America. And because I love America, in this time of war, I feel I have to now stand aside for our party and for our country.

—Conservative Political Action Conference,
Washington, D.C., February 7, 2008

6

HEALTH CARE

COST CONTROLS

Cost controls just don't work. We need to get health care to work more like a market, where the patient and the doctor have entirely different incentives than they do right now.

—*Talk of the Nation*, National Public Radio, March 3, 2010

GOVERNMENT MANDATE

I would not mandate at the federal level that every state do what we do, but what I would say at the federal level is we'll keep giving you these special payments we make if you adopt plans that get everybody insured. I want to get everybody insured. In Governor Schwarzenegger's state, he's got a different plan to get people insured. I wouldn't tell him he has to do it my way, but I'd say each state needs to get busy on the job of getting all our citizens insured. It does not cost more money.

—GOP presidential debate,
Manchester, New Hampshire, January 5, 2008

GOVERNMENT'S ROLE

Well, government plays a role. But the right answer in health care right now is not to say how do we put more government into it with more controls and regulations. That stops innovation. The right way to fix health care is to say how do we get it to act more like a consumer-driven free choice market. How do we get government out of it, if you will? And government has to play the role of making it more like a market. But encourage the right kinds of incentives so doctors and hospitals and patients do the right thing. When you have, what, 38, 40 percent of Americans obese and overweight, we got a problem with incentives.

—*Larry King Live*, CNN, December 3, 2009

HEALTH INSURANCE

Here's my view: If somebody can afford insurance and decides not to buy it and then they get sick, they ought to pay their own way as opposed to expect the government to pay their way, and that's an American principle. That's a principle of personal responsibility.

—GOP presidential debate,
Manchester, New Hampshire, January 5, 2008

Referring to RomneyCare: I want to make sure that every child has health insurance. As a matter of fact, I want to make sure every American has health insurance, not the Democratic way, not with the government handing out free insurance. That old joke by P. J. O'Rourke, he said, "If you think health care is expensive now, just wait till it's free." So, I'm not planning that. Instead, I believe that helping people get private free-market insurance is the way to go. We did that in our state.

—Campaign event, Orlando, Florida, January 21, 2008

INCENTIVES

America's health care is expensive because the incentives are all wrong—for the patient, the doctor, the hospital, and the insurer. Health care can't function like a market if it doesn't have incentives like a market. Fixing health care begins with fixing incentives.

—*No Apology*, by Mitt Romney, 2010

MEDICAID

In the same way that by cutting welfare spending dramatically, I don't think we hurt the poor. In the same way, I think cutting Medicaid spending by having it go to the states, run more efficiently with less fraud, I don't think will hurt the people that depend on that program for their health care.

—*Fox News Sunday* with Chris Wallace,
Fox News Channel, December 18, 2011

MEDICAL MARIJUANA

I've watched my wife's mom and dad, both in our home, [who] were going through cancer treatment, suffering a great deal of pain. But they didn't have marijuana, and they didn't need marijuana because there were other sources of pain management that worked entirely effectively. I'm told there is even a synthetic marijuana as well that's available.

—Campaign event,
Manchester, New Hampshire, October 4, 2007

When confronted about the use of medical marijuana by a young man sitting in a wheelchair who has muscular dystrophy: I am not in favor of medical marijuana being legal in the country.

—Campaign event,
Dover, New Hampshire, October 6, 2007

MEDICARE

Tomorrow's Medicare should give beneficiaries a generous defined contribution and allow them to choose between private plans and traditional Medicare. And lower-income future retirees should receive the most assistance. I believe that competition will improve Medicare and the coverage that seniors receive.

—*USA Today*, November 3, 2011

Republicans are talking about how to preserve Medicare and make sure it's an option for people down the road and make it fiscally sustainable. I don't know anyone among Republicans who is talking about cutting it. The only person who's cut Medicare for current Medicare recipients, is President Obama.

—Interview with *The Des Moines Register*
editorial board, December 9, 2011

OBAMACARE

This is not about getting competition in health insurance, which is already there. This is instead a Trojan horse. Barack Obama, when he ran for office, said he's in favor of a single-payer system. He's said it for years. This is a way of getting government into the insurance business so they can take over health care. It's the wrong way to go. And every single Republican and every thinking Democrat who knows something about the private sector would realize the wrong thing for America is to get government into the health-care business.

—This Week with George Stephanopoulos,
ABC News, June 14, 2009

It's filled with so many defects it's hard to know where exactly to begin. I'd say from a process standpoint the idea of rushing through a piece of legislation which will define the health-care system for this country is a very bad idea. The right approach is one which includes extensive analysis, evaluation of systems that have been implemented in other countries and in other states, a bipartisan effort which includes different perspectives and views, the inputs of physicians, patients, advocacy groups, hospitals, business, and labor. President Obama, out of an apparent desire to score a victory, is not willing to give health care the deliberative process it deserves.

—Human Events, July 30, 2009

His raises taxes; mine didn't. His cuts Medicare; mine didn't. His is done at a federal level; mine is done at a state-by-state level. So, in those three elements alone, it's a dramatically different plan. The idea that we're going to add another entitlement in a nation that's overwhelmed right now with entitlement liability—we didn't do that in Massachusetts.

—Weekend Edition Sunday,
National Public Radio, March 7, 2010

It's going to be a backbreaker on the U.S. economy.

—Larry King Live, CNN, March 23, 2010

If I am elected president, I will issue on my first day in office an executive order paving the way for waivers from ObamaCare for all 50 states. Subsequently, I will call on Congress to fully repeal ObamaCare.

—USA Today, May 11, 2011

Health care is more than just one-sixth of the American economy. It is a source of well-being for individuals and families. We are blessed with much that is good in American health care. But we have taken a turn for the worse with ObamaCare, with its high taxes and vastly expanded federal control over our lives. I believe the better course is to empower the states to determine their own health care futures.

—USA Today, May 11, 2011

ROMNEYCARE

There really wasn't Republican or Democrat in this. People ask me if this is conservative or liberal, and my answer is yes. It's liberal in the sense that we're getting our citizens health insurance. It's conservative in that we're not getting a government takeover.

—*New York Times*, April 5, 2006

If you can't afford—yes, if you can't afford anything, then we help subsidize the purchase of your insurance plan. So let's say you're earning two times federal poverty which, in my state, would be roughly $35,000 a year. In that case, you're going to be paying about $15 a week for your insurance. We'll pick up the remainder. And so the state picks up some portion of the insurance premium to make sure that everybody has a plan they can afford and it's not a government plan. Again, it's a private plan offered by the many insurance companies that compete here.

—*Hardball* with Chris Matthews, MSNBC, April 12, 2006

We're now spending, as a government, a billion dollars giving out free health care. We're collecting revenues from various parties to put in a pool to give out free health care to people who don't have health insurance. That's big government. Now we're saying you know what? No more. Now we're going to insist that people buy their own insurance if they can afford to do so. So we're doing our best to shrink government. We're not going to be adding employees. We're reducing the scale of government. And more importantly, we're saying no longer is government going to hand out free care. Now individuals are going to have responsibility for their own health insurance and we're going to keep from passing the burden of that coverage on to others. No more free riders.

—Charlie Rose, PBS, June 5, 2006

What we found was one-quarter of the uninsured in my state were making $75,000 a year or more, and my view is they should either buy insurance or they should pay their own way with a health savings account or some other savings account.

—GOP presidential debate,
Manchester, New Hampshire, January 5, 2008

It's the difference between a racehorse and a donkey, if you will. So, they both have four legs, but one works pretty well and the other's not working and would not work at all.

—Fox News Sunday with Chris Wallace,
Fox News Channel, March 7, 2010

Referring to his statements that the federal government funds 50 percent of the Massachusetts health-care plan: It was not a new burden on the federal government. It was a redirection of what they've been doing before.

—The O'Reilly Factor, Fox News Channel, April 12, 2010

Our plan was a state solution to a state problem. And his is a power grab by the federal government to put in place a one-size-fits-all plan across the nation.

—Presentation on Healthcare Reform,
Ann Arbor, Michigan, May 12, 2011

I also note, there's no government insurance here. We didn't create a government insurance program or a government policy that people got. No, no, we gave people a premium support program where they could buy their own private insurance of their choice, and for the poor, we helped them with support.

—Presentation on Healthcare Reform,
Ann Arbor, Michigan, May 12, 2011

Commenting on whether or not he should apologize for creating RomneyCare: I also recognize that a lot of pundits around the nation are saying that I should just stand up and say, "This whole thing was a mistake, that it was a boneheaded idea, and I should just admit it, it was a mistake, and walk away from it." And I presume that a lot of folks would conclude that if I did that, that it'd be good for me politically. But there's only one problem with that: it wouldn't be honest. I in fact did what I believed was right for the people of my state.

—Presentation on Healthcare Reform,
Ann Arbor, Michigan, May 12, 2011

TORT REFORM

The American Medical Association puts the number for defensive medicine at $200 billion. This is staggering waste. Defensive medicine also leads to unnecessary treatments that carry risk to the patient. Reforms that limit non-economic damages, assign malpractice cases to special health courts, and provide awards or indemnity according to a predetermined schedule can reduce the burden and ought to be widely implemented; states like Mississippi, Texas, and California are models. What prevents the adoption of malpractice reform, of course, is the massive financial contribution of the trial lawyers to the Democratic Party. This truly is an example of putting profits ahead of people.

—*No Apology*, by Mitt Romney, 2010

7

HIS LIFE

2002 WINTER OLYMPICS

Money and branding: They are part of the Olympics. But in my view, they are not at the heart of what the Olympics is about. In my view, the Olympics is the most effective platform for celebrating character on the world stage. The Olympians are real heroes in many cases, and the Olympics reveals their heroism to our kids and to the population of the world. And there are Olympic moments which are memorialized forever in the psyche of the world population, which affect how we think about ourselves and how we think about others. They inspire us. They lift us as a nation. They lift us towards peace and other notable lofty endeavors.

—National Press Club Newsmaker Luncheon,
Washington, D.C., February 3, 2000

I mean, it's one of the great ironies that someone with so little athletic ability as myself is actually involved in the Olympics. My sons actually pointed out that there is no conceivable circumstance under which they would have been able to predict that I would appear on the front page of the sports section.

—National Press Club Newsmaker Luncheon,
Washington, D.C., February 3, 2000

Regarding his wife encouraging him to become the Olympics CEO:
She told me, "You have exactly the background." The more I thought about it, I realized, we're only here for one lifetime. I was making more money than I should have. It was time to do something different.

—*New York Times*, September 24, 2000

I knew nothing about the United States Olympic Committee.
The only thing I read on the sports pages were the results.

—*New York Times*, September 24, 2000

In Salt Lake, hundreds of millions of dollars were spent by the
federal, state, and local governments and SLOC to secure the
Games. Literally thousands of people—cops, soldiers, firemen,
federal agents, public health workers, and volunteers—put
in hundreds of thousands of hours in harsh weather and cold
to keep the Games safe. Was that investment worth it? Absolutely. Because the Olympics also carries the dreams we have
of a world at peace—the world we are trying to create for our
grandchildren and those who come after. It is a dream shared
by all nations who send their finest to compete in the Olympics. And it is a dream we saw and felt on February 8, 2002,
when, in spite of the threat of terrorism, every nation invited to
our Games still sent their Olympic team and the athletes of the
world marched together into opening ceremonies.

—Congressional testimony on security at Olympic Games, May 4, 2004

ALCOHOL AND CIGARETTES

Never had drinks or tobacco. It's a religious thing. I tasted a beer and tried a cigarette once, as a wayward teenager, and never did again.

—People, December 5, 2011

BOOK, *NO APOLOGY:*
THE CASE FOR
AMERICAN GREATNESS

Well, actually, it's been in the works for a long time. I've done a lot of travel when I was in the business world and I've been very, very concerned about the direction our country is headed compared to other nations in the world. And I'm afraid that Washington politicians have put America on a road to decline. And this is, in effect, a wake-up call. I don't expect it to sell hundreds of thousands, millions of copies, but I expect opinion leaders to pick it up and take a read, and hopefully, we can get America on a course of greatness again. And I think that's in the cards. I think that'll happen. But we're going to throw out some of the ideas that are currently in ascendancy in Washington today.

—*On the Record w/Greta Van Susteren,*
Fox News Channel, January 8, 2010

At the same time, the broader purpose of this book is to describe my view that America is facing some real challenges. That's our overspending, our overdependence on foreign oil, the weakness in our schools, the weakness in the foundations of our national proactivity and economy, the atrophy that is occurring in some parts of our military. It's not going to be easy, but the tough road ahead typically makes us stronger.

—*Weekend Edition Sunday,*
National Public Radio, March 7, 2010

CARS

Someday when I have the time to fuss with a car that's temperamental and needs repair all the time I might think about an old Mustang or an old Corvette. I would love to get an early 1950s vintage Corvette.

—Remarks at a gas station while filling up his campaign bus in Randolph, New Hampshire, December 22, 2011

FAMILY

Some people bring work home. They eat dinner and then they go into the study and work. When I came home, I put the briefcase by the door and didn't look at it till the next morning. For me, life is what happens away from work. Life is about family. I recognize that if I get elected to the office I seek, family time will be dramatically cut back. It will be my time to serve.

—*Parade*, December 4, 2011

FATHER

My dad [George Romney], I mean, I am a small shadow of the real deal. My dad was extraordinary.

—*This Week* with George Stephanopoulos,
ABC News, February 18, 2007

The older I get, the smarter Dad is. I pattern myself like him— his character, his sense of vision, his sense of purpose.

—*Time*, May 21, 2007

My father never graduated from college. He apprenticed as a lath and plaster carpenter, and he was darn good at it. He used to brag that he could put a handful of nails in his mouth and spit them out, pointed nail end first. And then on his honeymoon, he and Mom drove across the country. Dad sold aluminum paint along the way, to pay for hotels and gas. But Dad always believed in America; and in that America, a lath and plaster man could work his way up to running a little car company called American Motors. And end up as governor of a state where he had once sold aluminum paint.

—Conservative Political Action Conference,
Washington, D.C., February 11, 2011

He was here running for president in 1968, and I hope I do better than he did.

—University of New Hampshire at Manchester, June 3, 2011

FOOD

I'm a person of streaks. For a while I had to have granola all the time. Now it's dried fruit, nuts, and peanut butter.

—*People*, December 5, 2011

HAIR

I saw just yesterday the chairman of Governor Huckabee's campaign said that he would like to knock my teeth out. My only comment on that is, don't touch the hair.

—Campaign event, Des Moines, Iowa, January 3, 2008

Joking about a minor fight he got into with rapper Sky Blu from LMFAO while they were on a plane: He gave a good swat—and broke my hair.

—*Late Show with David Letterman,* CBS, March 2, 2010

After being pressed by host Mike Barnicle on whether his hair is real: I glued this on this morning. It's not moving.

—*Morning Joe,* MSNBC, March 3, 2010

Romney's number-one thing on his top ten things he'd like to get off his chest: It's a hairpiece.

—*Late Show with David Letterman,* CBS, December 19, 2011

LEADERSHIP

There's a big difference between pontificating and speaking and actually leading. And over the last thirty or thirty-five years, I've had the experience of being a leader. I've run things. I've built teams. I've been able to make differences, not just talk about differences, but make differences that affected the lives of individuals.

—Campaign event, Iowa, January 2, 2008

THE LIGHTHEARTED MITT

I love practical jokes and humor. That there's frankly no joke that I don't think is funny. I love practical jokes, but I don't like being scared. My sons will tell you that when they have jumped out of the tree when I'm coming from work in the middle of the night and said "boo" to me, that there is swift and severe retribution.

—*RealClearPolitics*, February 23, 2007

At the event I was at yesterday, Santa Claus arrived, all dressed up in a beautiful Santa outfit, full-flowing white beard. And he asked me what I wanted for Christmas and I said, well, I want Iowa, New Hampshire . . . Wyoming, South Carolina, Michigan. And I'd love to have your help.

—Campaign event, Spartanburg, South Carolina, December 18, 2007

Why are there so many beautiful women here? I haven't figured this out. Cuban American women are gorgeous.

—Campaign event, Sweetwater, Florida, January 27, 2008

After my own campaign was over, Ann and I just wanted to get away from it all. We ended up in Beijing, about as far away as you can get. We went to the Olympic Games, and one of the events we attended was women's beach volleyball. I noticed a lot of people looking in our direction, pointing toward us and taking pictures. It's always nice to be recognized, and I told Ann, "Let's be sure to smile and look our best." Ann said, "They might like us even more if we got out of the way—Kobe Bryant is standing right behind you."

—House Republican Conference Retreat, January 30, 2009

After eating Gino's East pizza with small business owners, Romney did not want any food to be wasted—so he had the leftovers delivered to President Obama's Chicago campaign headquarters. A campaign source confirmed that the pizza was in fact delivered there: Great deep dish at @ginoseast. Sending the extra slices to @barackobama and his Chicago HQ team.

—Twitter: @MittRomney, May 26, 2011

I saw the young man over there with eggs Benedict, with hollandaise sauce with the eggs there. And I was going to suggest to you that you serve your eggs with hollandaise sauce in hubcaps. Because there's no plates like chrome for the hollandaise.

—Campaign event,
Manchester, New Hampshire, June 14, 2011

I'll always make light of myself, and self-deprecating humor is part of who I am.

—Campaign event, Smyrna, Georgia, June 16, 2011

Contrasting himself with Barack Obama, who is portrayed as regularly using a teleprompter: Now, this is going to be a conversation today. I don't have a text written. You can actually see here what I've got. I've got notes. All right? I've got some notes of some things I want to tell you. I'm not going to be reading and I don't have a teleprompter here. Nothing wrong with that. I use it from time to time.

—Campaign event,
North Las Vegas, Nevada, September 6, 2011

LIVING WISELY

Over the years, I have watched a good number of people live out their lives in the shallows. In the shallows, life is all about yourself. Your job, your money, your house, your rights, your needs, your opinions, your ideas, your comfort. In the deeper waters, life is about others: family, friends, faith, community, country, caring, commitment. In the deeper waters, there are challenging ideas, opposing opinions, and uncomfortable battles. One business colleague, I'll call Rich, told me that his life ambition was to be listed in *Forbes* among the four hundred wealthiest people in the world. His ambition, his preoccupation with self, overshadowed his marriage and his loyalties to his friends—so he lost them all. He became wealthy in the way he hoped. But he swims in the shallowest of waters, because he swims alone.

—Commencement address, Suffolk University,
Boston, Massachusetts, May 23, 2004

We live "lives of quiet desperation" unless we reach for something that is as meaningful as it is unexpected. Linear, logical, focused careers may not be so logical after all. The predictable path can be constraining, limiting, hardening.

—*Turnaround: Crisis, Leadership, and the Olympic Games*,
Mitt Romney with Timothy Robinson, 2007

MASSACHUSETTS

We've lived here now 34 years, raised all five of our sons here, and paid a mountain of taxes here. You don't do that unless you enjoy the state and the economic, social, and cultural opportunities which it provides.

—*American Spectator*, March 2006

My dream was to be the head of a big automobile company. I hoped to be head of Ford or American Motors or General Motors, and that was what I thought my future would hold. When I moved to Massachusetts I got involved in the private sector. It was very exciting and I presumed I would always be in the private sector. Had I thought politics was in my future, I would not have chosen Massachusetts as the state of my residence. I would have stayed in Michigan where my dad's name was golden.

—*American Spectator*, March 2006

I came into a state that was in real trouble—a huge budget gap, losing jobs every month. We turned it around. Three out of four years, we had [an] unemployment rate below the national average, we ended up with [a] 4.7 percent unemployment rate. I'm proud of what we were able to do in a tough situation.

—GOP presidential debate,
Simi Valley, California, September 7, 2011

In 2003, I became governor of a state hobbled by a deficit and shedding jobs as it came out of a recession. Working with a legislature under solid (85 percent!) Democratic control, I cut taxes 19 times, reformed and reorganized state government, and balanced the budget four years in a row. By the time I left office, Massachusetts employers were once again hiring, and the state had a rainy-day surplus of $2 billion.

—Mittromney.com, September 29, 2011

MISSIONARY WORK

On a mission, your faith in Jesus Christ either evaporates or it becomes much deeper. For me it became much deeper.

—*New York Times*, November 14, 2007

There were surely times on my mission when I was having a particularly difficult time accomplishing very little when I would have longed for the chance to be serving in the military, but that was not to be.

—*New York Times*, November 14, 2007

SONS

I am delighted that each of my sons are following their hearts in different directions. If they wanted to get into politics that would be fine, but it is a rough road. I would just ask that they get into politics to do something, not to be somebody.

—*Campaigns & Elections*, August 2007

STYLE

My favorite item of apparel for a man is to be able to have a nice necktie, it's the only thing with color and interest that I have. But you know I don't wear neckties all the time, I do when I go to church, I do at fundraisers or formal events, but if I'm with the family or at a farm like I am today, you know, you dress like I'm at a farm.

—ABCNews.com, June 2, 2011

THANKSGIVING

We will typically begin with football—that's the boys, at least. And we have a couple of neighbors that we have a football game with. Then we typically watch the Detroit Lions games. It used to be always with the Green Bay Packers, but my family tradition is to watch the Lions. And then we have an overstuffed turkey. I typically overstuff it, which makes it cook too long and get too dry, but that's how it works. Actually, the day begins with Ann and I coming down and preparing the turkey. And I usually do the stuffing and pack it in too tight, as I've indicated. She gets all the other parts of the meal together.

—News conference, November 19, 2007

TRANSPARENCY

As Popeye used to say, "I am what I am." I'm as clear as I can be to people as to what my views are. . . . When I ran for office I indicated I did not favor same-sex marriage or civil unions and I have simply stood by that position. . . . At the same time, I've indicated I'm a person who will follow the law. I respect the process of the law and if the legal processes result in a conclusion I disagree with, I will nonetheless follow the law. I swore to do that when I became governor. A lot of what is passed by the legislature is not as I would pass it, but I will implement it and enforce it.

—*American Spectator*, March 2006

WIFE

·

Referring to Thanksgiving: She's the cook, I'm the sous chef.

—News conference, November 19, 2007

Now, Ann here has been campaigning all over the country. She is a remarkable, tireless woman, who has great capacity. And the amazing thing is that she gets along with me after all these years, and it's been a long, long time, I tell you, from her standpoint. From mine, it seems like just yesterday that I went to Cindy White's house for a party—this was my senior year in high school—and there was a girl I had known in elementary school, a couple of grades beneath me there. You know, in elementary school, if they're two grades beneath you, why, they're like a child. So as a fourth grader, you think a second grader is a child. And so I didn't really pay much attention to Ann in elementary school, but when she was just turning sixteen, I found her very interesting. And so she was at that party and I came up and said hello to her and got to know her a little bit better, and then I went to her date, who had brought her to the party, and I said, "You know, I live closer to Ann's house than you do and I wonder if I can give her a ride home for you," and we've been going steady ever since. And she is the mother of our five sons, mom also to five daughters-in-law and eleven grandchildren, the love of my life. And I love to tell this story, because we've been going together so long. When we got into this race, and you may have heard this, I told her, "Sweetheart, in your wildest dreams, did you see me running for president of the United States?" And she said, "Mitt, you weren't in my wildest dreams."

—Remarks after Nevada Caucus results,
January 19, 2008

I got a letter toward the end of my mission saying she'd met someone she liked, though not as much as me. So I was pleased when I saw her waiting at the airport with our families. Immediately we knew we still had the same feelings for each other. On the ride home, she and I were in the third row of this station wagon. I said, "Do you want to get married?" She answered, "Absolutely."

—*Parade*, December 4, 2011

I think she has more confidence in me than I have in myself. She believed that my business experiences in start-ups and turnarounds, in the Olympics, and as a Republican governor in a Democratic state prepared me uniquely to help the country in a troubled time. And that I have a responsibility to serve. As she calls on that sense of duty, I'm defenseless.

—*Parade*, December 4, 2011